MYSTERY AND MYTH
IN THE PHILOSOPHY OF
ERIC VOEGELIN

MYSTERY AND MYTH
IN THE PHILOSOPHY OF
ERIC VOEGELIN

· Glenn Hughes ·

UNIVERSITY OF MISSOURI PRESS

COLUMBIA AND LONDON

5   4   3   2   1   97   96   95   94   93

Permission to quote from the following works of Eric Voegelin has been granted by
Louisiana State University Press: *Order and History,* vol. 1, *Israel and Revelation,*
© 1956; *Order and History,* vol. 4, *The Ecumenic Age,* © 1974; *The Collected
Works of Eric Voegelin,* vol. 12, *Published Essays, 1966–1985,* ed. Ellis Sandoz,
© 1990; *The Collected Works of Eric Voegelin,* vol. 23, *What Is History? and Other
Late Unpublished Writings,* ed. Thomas A. Hollweck and Paul Caringella, © 1990.

A version of chapter 3 was published as "Eric Voegelin's View of History as a Drama
of Transfiguration" in *International Philosophical Quarterly,* 1990, no. 1, and is
reprinted by permission.

Library of Congress Cataloging-in-Publication Data

Hughes, Glenn, 1951–
    Mystery and myth in the philosophy of Eric Voegelin / Glenn Hughes.
        p.   cm.
    Includes bibliographical references and index.
    ISBN 0-8262-0875-4 (alk. paper)
    1. Voegelin, Eric, 1901-   .   2. Consciousness—History—20th century.
3. Mysticism.   I. Title
B3354.V884H84   1993
193—dc20   92-34192
                                                                    CIP

∞™ This paper meets the requirements of the
American National Standard for Permanence of Paper
for Printed Library Materials, Z39.48, 1984.

Designer: *Kristie Lee*
Typesetter: *Connell-Zeko Type & Graphics*
Printer and Binder: *Thomson-Shore, Inc.*
Typefaces: *Sabon and Belwe Light*

For Tom McPartland

Guard the Mysteries!
Constantly reveal Them!
—LEW WELCH

CONTENTS

· 4 ·

ACKNOWLEDGMENTS

This book originated as a doctoral dissertation written at Boston College under the direction of Professor Frederick Lawrence, whose knowledge and love of Voegelin's work set the pattern. I am indebted both to him and to Professor Patrick Byrne for guidance, as well as for the spirit of generosity with which they embraced the project. While writing I was greatly helped and encouraged by the insights of my friends Sebastian Moore, O.S.B.; Professor Paul Kidder; Pat Brown; and Professor Paulette Kidder. In addition I owe thanks to the following individuals who, in ways direct and indirect, helped me to bring the work to completion: Katharine Anderson; Joseph Flanagan, S.J.; Bill Gray; Mark Hart; Jim Marshall; Eric McVittie; William Richardson, S.J.; Bill Stevenson; and Tova Wein.

MYSTERY AND MYTH
IN THE PHILOSOPHY OF
ERIC VOEGELIN

INTRODUCTION

The aim of this book is to analyze and relate the many discussions of mystery that run as a persistent theme through the writings of Eric Voegelin. A refined appreciation of mystery is, for Voegelin, one of the requirements for being a true philosopher. The apperception and acceptance of elemental mysteries is a necessary condition, in his view, for the proper formation of individual character, as well as for the development of adequate social viewpoints and political policies. Nor is the critical or explicit knowledge of just where human understanding finds itself confronted and contained by irreducible mysteries an achievement to be taken for granted in human affairs. On the contrary, it has been a hard-won and precious advance in the struggle for human self-understanding. As Voegelin emphasizes at the start of his five-volume masterwork, *Order and History,* human beings "can achieve considerable knowledge about the order of being, and not the least part of that knowledge is the distinction between the knowable and the unknowable."[1]

Voegelin holds that we have experienced, during the last few centuries in the West, a peculiar and growing eclipse of the awareness of mystery. Various causes may be traced. Many leading figures of the Enlightenment, as a part of their fight against Church authority, made respect for mystery taboo. Meanwhile, the growing power of the modern natural sciences both in speculative reach and technological invention began to

---

1. *Order and History,* vol. 1, *Israel and Revelation,* 2. All references to *Order and History* that follow will be to titles of individual volumes: vol. 2, *The World of the Polis;* vol. 3, *Plato and Aristotle;* vol. 4, *The Ecumenic Age;* and vol. 5, *In Search of Order.*

nourish a widespread conviction that the universe could not for long hold back any of its secrets from the human mind. These are just two of numerous factors contributing to the loss of sensitivity toward mystery in our everyday, pre-reflective orientation within reality—an orientation involving not only the dominance of certain moods, outlooks, and convictions in society but also the decision making that determines political, cultural, and educational policies. For Voegelin, the decline of our awareness of and respect for mystery is intimately connected both with the widespread existential malaise and with the political horror stories of the twentieth century. This is why in his writings on political, historical, and philosophical themes he returns again and again to the topic of mystery.

It will be helpful to clarify at the outset what Voegelin means by *mystery*. Like Gabriel Marcel, what Voegelin calls mystery is not merely a blank of unknowability facing reason in its effort to expand its holdings, but rather a characteristic of human existence, of the human situation. In other words, it doesn't simply confront us; it defines us. "A mystery," writes Marcel, "is something in which I am myself involved." Thus, in his oft-quoted distinction, a mystery is not simply a "problem," something facing me, which may even be insoluble, but which doesn't implicate me in its dilemma and in relation to which I myself remain "in a non-problematical sphere." A mystery is something known to be unknowable that pertains to existence itself, making it an unknown that, in some inescapable way, I am. The notion of mystery, as Marcel puts it, introduces "a sphere where the distinction between what is in me and what is before me loses its meaning and its initial validity."[2]

Voegelin's use of the term *mystery* harmonizes with that of Marcel. The mysteries about which Voegelin writes are depths of meaning whose hiddenness is apparent, and which could be known fully only if reality as a whole were known, while the human knower remains a participant in reality with a limited perspective, unable to fully penetrate the meanings that constitute human existence. Therefore, the unknowns in which we find our lives to be totally implicated are not problems to be solved or

2. *Being and Having: An Existentialist Diary,* 117; *Man Against Mass Society,* 89. On Marcel's distinction between "problem" and "mystery," see his *Being and Having,* 116–23; *Man Against Mass Society,* 89–92; and *The Mystery of Being,* vol. 1, *Reflection and Mystery,* 260–70.

not solved, but mysteries to be lived and, so that they may be lived freely and graciously, constantly revealed.

As mentioned, Voegelin perceives modern culture in the West to be sadly and dangerously lacking in consistently balanced awareness of the mysterious dimension of conscious existence—the basic mysteries having, as he might put it, slipped below the level of public consciousness. His philosophy, like Marcel's, has as one of its aims the critical recognition of these forgotten truths, marking "a philosopher's resistance to the distortion and destruction" caused by the dominance in the West of intellectual premises and pragmatic policies no longer rooted in a balanced appreciation of the limits of human knowing. But he goes beyond Marcel, and indeed any other contemporary philosopher, in the extent of his diagnosis of the historical circumstances that in the West have led to what he portrays as the current state of "imaginative oblivion" with respect to the mysteries of reality.[3] The quality of that diagnosis derives largely from a concern with the intricacies of the philosophical problem of transcendence—a central topic of the following chapters. As we shall see, for Voegelin the explicit discovery of transcendent meaning in the course of the human search for truth has introduced problems of such magnitude that we are still struggling with them, mostly unsuccessfully, in every important dimension of personal and political life.

Now, while mystery is emphatically an existential notion, it remains also a cognitional notion. It refers to something human knowing is aware of but cannot comprehend: a known unknown.[4] Therefore, the foundation for a convincing philosophical examination of the basic human mysteries must include a general theory of human knowledge or consciousness. And Voegelin's philosophy is, in fact, built upon an explicit, detailed analysis of the nature of consciousness. He makes clear that the principles of his work as a philosopher lie in his theory of consciousness, which, in the final analysis, provides justification for his political and historical interpretations. Throughout his career he continued to refine that theory, understanding it as the key to his life's work.[5]

3. *The Ecumenic Age,* 335; *In Search of Order,* 41–43, 61–62.

4. Mystery as a "known unknown" is discussed in Bernard J. F. Lonergan, *Insight: A Study of Human Understanding,* 531–49.

5. For this decisive assessment, see the foreword, written by Voegelin's widow, Lissy, to *In Search of Order.* The major elements of Voegelin's theory of consciousness

the purely passive spectator = absolute self i.e. "OUTSIDE" of reality
which is foolish.

vs. the knowing subj. as a purely passive
spectator ("Spirit of American Philo") p. 199 p. 230
p. 195 (bottom) p. 228 p. 231
207 top 208
(212)

To describe a philosopher on the contemporary scene as one whose work is built upon a "theory of consciousness" invites the suspicion that he has either missed, or is fighting a rearguard action against, what might be called the hermeneutical revolution. In current philosophical debate, concern with the act of interpretation and the structure of language (signs) has largely replaced the concern to establish a foundational philosophy of "consciousness" or "mind," the latter dismissed as a misguided adventure having had its raison d'être in fallacious Cartesian and Idealist assumptions that there is something like an "absolute subject" that can become, at least to some degree, rationally "transparent" to itself. Indeed, the prevailing tendency is to reject the quest for "foundations" of any sort. A thinker like Voegelin, then, appears to be guilty of philosophical naïveté.

Thus a word must be said about what Voegelin means by "theory of consciousness," since with its associations the phrase is unfortunately misleading. What Voegelin means by *consciousness* is not the formal structure of an absolute subject, but a kind of participation in reality. Acts of consciousness, as participation, must be conceived from two points of view simultaneously. From one point of view, consciousness indeed belongs, as the besieged tradition would have it, to an intentional subject, bodily founded, a subject who can claim authorship of intentional operations, deliberative thought and action, and the "project" of individuality. From another perspective, however, and at the same time, consciousness is an element "given" within reality, and as such it "belongs" to the reality in which it has appeared or irrupted. In other words, as Voegelin has put it, the conscious subject is also a "predicative event" in the process of reality, the ultimate subject of which—to extend a metaphor—is the mysterious ground of all things.[6] Consciousness, therefore, is neither a subject nor a non-subject; it is both subject *and* non-subject, both author and event.

---

are to be found in his *Anamnesis* (American edition) and *In Search of Order.* The American edition of *Anamnesis* differs in content from the German original, *Anamnesis: Zur Theorie der Geschichte und Politik;* two new chapters were added, and some of the essays in the original were omitted. The new design enabled the American edition to be structured more tightly around Voegelin's work on a theory of consciousness. All further references to *Anamnesis* will be to the American edition.

6. *In Search of Order,* 15–16.

Voegelin is perhaps unique among philosophers in his insistence on keeping both of these aspects of consciousness in view when interpreting political and historical meaning. As a consequence, he is not guilty of the reifying of consciousness and the absolutizing of the subject, in the manner of modern rationalist philosophers from Descartes to Husserl, so intensively critiqued since the late nineteenth century and most radically by postmodernists such as Derrida and Lyotard; but neither is he willing to abandon the subject of intentional acts, the responsible author of interpretations, decisions, and actions, to the status of a sort of puppet ruled by the arbitrary "play" of impersonal linguistic or other structures. For Voegelin, the notions of "absolute subject" and "disembodied reason" attacked by Nietzsche, Heidegger, Derrida, and others do indeed represent a distortion of human experience, because they suffer from blindness to, or resistance against recognizing, the primary "not-I" of consciousness as an event and a given. But he would reject their call for a radical rejection of all "anthropologism" as an extreme position that ignores that the "event-ing" of consciousness does not negate the presence of an intentional subject—unless one adheres to a strict logic of exclusion. Voegelin admits readily that to assert that one and the same consciousness is both I and not-I, both subject and predicate, is a "paradox."[7] He is most willing to assert that a sound theory of consciousness must embrace this *coincidentia oppositorum*. And he is quick to criticize writings that appear to ignore, or to emphasize too exclusively, either of these co-constituting dimensions of consciousness.

No more than Voegelin is unaware of the problems of absolutizing the subject is he insensitive to the priority of problems of language and interpretation. Language symbols, as he calls them, must be recognized as inherently unstable, both because all horizons of linguistic meaning are contingent and because a sharp distinction must always be made between meaning intended and meaning conveyed. The struggle to find and apply a method for interpreting important texts in a manner that recognizes the intrinsic uncertainties and incompleteness of the task, while at the same time securing a confident ballast of meaning, preoccupied Voegelin in his philosophical work. The hermeneutical principles at which he arrived, including his leading rule of distinguishing between

7. Ibid., 14–18.

language symbols and the experiences that engender them, and his practice of "meditative exegeses" of experiences underlying the formation of key symbols or terms, are discussed throughout his writings, evidence that he, too, has made the "linguistic turn."[8]

How Voegelin developed his hermeneutical methods, under what pressure of circumstances, and what specific inadequacies they were intended to correct have been discussed in the introductory accounts of his work and career by Eugene Webb and Ellis Sandoz. These works and others supply the introductory expositions on the origins, outlook, and achievements of Voegelin's philosophy that otherwise would be required here in order to analyze in some detail his philosophy of mystery.[9] Some specific areas of Voegelin's work have received persistent critical treatment, as for example his interpretations of biblical texts and traditions and the theological implications of his writings. The topic of mystery, however, while a prominent theme in Voegelin's work (along with the related topic of myth), has received relatively little critical attention.[10] This is due in part to the necessarily supportive, though crucial, role it plays in the examination of major thinkers and of symbols of political and existential order that make up the bulk of Voegelin's writings. Though never itself the subject of sustained analysis by Voegelin himself,

8. On Voegelin's principle of distinguishing between symbol and engendering experience, see his "Equivalences of Experience and Symbolization in History"; "Immortality: Experience and Symbol," 52–54; *Autobiographical Reflections,* 93–97; and *Anamnesis,* 11–12. The most helpful description of the process of meditative exegesis is found in Voegelin, "The Beginning and the Beyond: A Meditation on Truth," 188–91.

9. Webb, *Eric Voegelin: Philosopher of History;* Sandoz, *The Voegelinian Revolution: A Biographical Introduction.* See also Barry Cooper, *The Political Theory of Eric Voegelin;* Eugene Webb, *Philosophers of Consciousness: Polanyi, Lonergan, Voegelin, Ricoeur, Girard, Kierkegaard,* 91–136; and the collections in Stephen A. McKnight, ed., *Eric Voegelin's Search for Order in History,* and Ellis Sandoz, ed., *Eric Voegelin's Thought: A Critical Appraisal.*

10. Some commentators have emphasized the centrality of mystery in Voegelin's philosophy and briefly discussed his position, although none has treated the topic at length. See Paul Caringella, "Eric Voegelin: Philosopher of Divine Presence"; John Carmody, "Noetic Differentiation: Religious Implications," 159–69; Denise Lardner Carmody and John Tully Carmody, "Voegelin and the Restoration of Order: A Meditation," 90–93; Russell Nieli, "Eric Voegelin's Evolving Ideas on Gnosticism, Mysticism, and Modern Radical Politics," 97–101; and Webb, *Philosophers of Consciousness,* 106–15.

it is a frequent theme, invoked and expounded for the purpose of reminding us of the discernible contours of the human situation and of
the fact of transcendent meaning. On inspection, Voegelin's analysis
of the mysteries of reality, and of the challenges and duties of appreciat-
ing them, plays a primary role in his overall philosophy, one that in some
ways binds together his theory of consciousness, his philosophy of history, the theological aspects of his work, and, ultimately, his views on
what constitutes political health and disease. The present book is an
attempt, then, to examine Voegelin's philosophy of mystery and also,
by showing how it pervades and shapes all the main areas of his thought,
to broaden the critical understanding of his philosophy as a whole.

The following account takes its structure from the need to first establish the principles upon which Voegelin's treatment of mystery rests, and
only afterward to offer a summary interpretation that knits together his
own widely scattered discussions and remarks on the topic. Accordingly,
the first two chapters address Voegelin's theory of consciousness, drawing out its implications for an understanding of basic mysteries. The first
chapter, "Theory of Consciousness," presents an overview of that theory,
tracing its development from theoretical breakthroughs in the early
1940s to the last formulations in the posthumous *In Search of Order*. The
chapter's purpose includes showing the fundamental consistency of his
increasingly nuanced analysis of consciousness over four decades and
his likewise consistent placement of ultimate questions, which are not
definitively answerable, at the center of human self-understanding. The
second chapter, "The Question of the Ground," examines in detail
Voegelin's all-important thesis of the differentiation of consciousness,
an event defined as involving, among other things, the conceptual differentiation of strictly transcendent reality. By approaching this complex
area of Voegelin's thought from the direction of the invariant thrust of
human consciousness toward an understanding of its own most elementary meaning (its "ground"), two things can be highlighted: (1) the
coherence of the thesis itself, as it founds both pre-differentiated consciousness and the differentiating processes upon an invariant core of
questioning awareness that naturally unfolds into a more discriminat-
ing (differentiated) understanding of its own structure and meaning and
(2) the inevitability of questioning consciousness, with its perspectival
limitations, coming to a more and more explicit recognition of just where

it is that human knowing encounters radical unknowability regarding the meanings that comprehend and confront it. Now, this differentiation of consciousness, which is in part a response to the fact of transcendent meaning, is at the heart of Voegelin's understanding of what constitutes "history." Therefore, in the third chapter, "The Drama of History," the preceding analysis is placed in the wider context of Voegelin's philosophy of history, and the relation of mystery to history is examined. And insofar as history encompasses the whole human story, this chapter also requires a more detailed continuation of the discussion, already begun in the first two chapters, of Voegelin's insistence on the general human need for mythic articulation of mysteries concerning both the whole of reality and the meaning of human participation in that whole. The culminating chapter, then, distills the fruits of these analyses and adds to them, in what is hoped is a clarification of the central elements in Voegelin's mystagogy, his teaching of mysteries. The chapter's title, "Mystery and Mythos," indicates as well the importance of Voegelin's philosophy of myth to his analysis of mystery and, indeed, to his entire thought.

A few words must be said about Voegelin's interest in myth. He is, of course, far from alone in his close interest in the topic, in his concern to rehabilitate myth as a healthy feature of human living, and in his lamenting the corrosive intolerance toward mythic symbolization that is characteristic of modernity, which has left us not, of course, in a mythless culture, but in a culture in which the guiding myths go unrecognized under various pseudorationalistic and pseudoscientific guises, myths that are neither helpful for mediating fundamental mysteries nor, because not recognized as myths, subject to the appropriate critical pressure. His company in this regard includes other philosophers as well as anthropologists, historians of religion, psychologists, sociologists, and creative artists. "No period since the early Renaissance," writes George Steiner, "has been more concerned with, has addressed itself more insistently to, the nature of the mythical than our own. Remythologization . . . may, in future, be seen as defining the spirit of the age."[11] This examination of myth and the mythic has been fueled in part by the accelerating breakdown in the West of confidence in all forms of system and certitude, whether scientific, philosophical, or religious. Myths offer an articula-

11. *Real Presences*, 221.

tion of ultimate concerns that is inherently "pluralistic" and "diverse," nonexclusive and not claiming unambiguous certainty, and therefore "democratic"—an attractive undermining of the exaggerated claims of intellectual mastery and dogmatic exclusivity.

Voegelin's understanding of the importance of myth differs, however, in significant ways from that of the majority of contemporary philosophers fascinated with the topic. While he too promotes the view that myth is central both to human self-understanding and to the current turbulent reorganization of cultural self-interpretation in the West, he does not see the recovery of myth as revolutionary action taken against the assumption that there exists transcendent meaning, nor as a salutary replacement of "metanarratives" by happily irresolvable personal narratives. Myths, for Voegelin, are not immanent fictions, nor are they loved for their pluralism alone. For him, they are of crucial value because their symbolic and narrative form can communicate mysteries—that is, truths of transcendent meaning that we can only know by way of analogy, or by means of intimation, as through a glass darkly. They are indeed necessary for the healthy discernment of the order of things because they satisfy the normative thrust of imagination for symbolic expression of its inherent awareness of both a supervening meaning in reality and the human incapacity to penetrate cognitively that meaning. Thus Voegelin upholds myth as a foil, not to an ultimately rational order of things (though he would claim that only trust, love, and faith can discern such an order), nor to the universality of scientific truth (for within the sphere of immanent structures, there are such truths), but to literalist and speculative accounts of transcendent meaning that transgress the limits of our actual knowledge, and to reductionists or "immanentists" who equate the meaningful with the world intrinsically conditioned by space and time.

In other words, unlike a number of the postmodern philosophers, Voegelin admires the open-endedness and multiformity of the myth, not because these are a guarantee of cognitive impotence, but because they reflect the open-endedness of transcendence. And he remains confident in myth's ability to genuinely and effectively mediate a transcendent realm of meaning that is one and enduring, though it is known only through the symbolic and existential fragmentariness of the human situation. Thus for Voegelin there are revelatory myths. They are stories or analogies that may claim the status of "truth" of a distinct kind. They do not supply certainty; yet they are "grounded," for the transcendent ground has, through the searching of human imagination, something to say.

The reader familiar with Voegelin's writings will notice that the following study focuses on the last thirty or so years of his writings, on his mature formulations and conclusions. There are discussions of the development of his thought with respect to both his theory of consciousness and his philosophy of history, discussions intrinsic to these subject matters insofar as Voegelin's philosophical work was always emphatically a search in progress rather than a search for system, but in general the study aims to be a synthetic and not a genetic account of the key topics. And finally, in the examination of a thinker who has been criticized and, to a sad degree, neglected due to his use of what is seen as an obscure and idiosyncratic terminology, an effort has been made to explain Voegelin not merely in his own terms (which is all too common in the critical literature) but also in a more universal and accessible philosophical language. It is hoped that in this way the precision and explanatory potency of his thought will have been made all the more obvious.

· 1 ·

THEORY OF CONSCIOUSNESS

An analysis of Eric Voegelin's theory of consciousness may well begin with a warning that it is not what a reader acquainted with modern philosophies of "consciousness" might be led to expect. It does not offer, for example, to explain in any detail the distinct operations or actions performed by the mind as it exercises its functions—it is not a cognitional theory or a psychology. Nor does it concern itself with how exactly understanding comes about, what judging is, and how we know that we know—it is not an epistemology. Neither is it an analysis of the powers and scope of reason in the manner of Kant's transcendental critique, nor of the various intentional acts by which a horizon of consciousness is constituted, as in Husserl's phenomenology of the "transcendental ego." What is it then?

Its closest cousin in modern philosophy is probably Heidegger's analysis of existence as Dasein, an analysis sustained by the insight, which can easily come to be regarded as the Archimedean principle of philosophizing itself, that human existence is where Being becomes reflectively aware of itself. Consciousness is, of course, something that belongs to a specific individual, concretely located in space and time. But it is also true to say that, since a person occurs in the course of Being, individual consciousness is also something that belongs to Being. And since Being comprehends or embraces individual consciousness, it might be given a certain priority over the individual as regards the determination of to whom, or to what, consciousness ultimately "belongs." Therefore,

11

Heidegger describes human awareness as, primordially, an illumination or "clearing" in Being, as a being-*there* (*Da-Sein*).[1]

Voegelin, like Heidegger, considers consciousness in terms of its broadest possible ontological meaning. He too specifies it as the site in finite existence where meaning itself is illuminated. Both philosophers further agree that the classical analysis of "human nature" has over the centuries tended to obscure what is distinctive about this mode of being through patterning its explanations on the model of statically conceived forms or artifacts, explanations that lend themselves to a conception of consciousness as one type of "thing" among others in the world. This reified, or hypostatized, conception of consciousness is precisely what Voegelin's theory, like Heidegger's notion of Dasein, is intended to subvert. Heidegger, indeed, would object that the very term *consciousness* (*Bewusstsein*) is, because of its use by the German Idealists, intractably suggestive of the mind conceived as a special kind of substance.[2] In this regard, Heidegger is more sensitive than Voegelin to the drawbacks of using a term like consciousness to describe what he is talking about. On the other hand, Voegelin's greater readiness to use conventional and custom-honored language to explain himself pays homage to the unoriginality of the truths about existence he purports to express. Unlike Heidegger, he does not see his philosophical perspective as revolutionary. In his view, the basic truths of consciousness about which he writes are perennially recognized, were first systematically expounded by Plato and Aristotle, and have continued to nourish philosophy even as they have been misunderstood, formulated in misleading ways, and set up as final "metaphysical doctrines" about a type of "thing" called "human nature." With respect to his work on consciousness, Voegelin writes: "The validating question will have to be: Do we have to ignore and eclipse a major part of the historical field, in order to maintain the truth of the propositions . . . or are the propositions recognizably equivalent with

1. The basic text for the analysis of Dasein is Martin Heidegger, *Being and Time.*
2. Heidegger, *Being and Time,* 72, 150. For Voegelin's treatment of the historical background to this problem, see his detailed analysis of the Greek origins of the idea of nature (*physis*) in *Anamnesis,* chapter 5, "What Is Nature?" 71–88, where he examines the dominance of the models of organism and artifact in Aristotle's interpretation of reality. For an introductory passage on the same topic by Heidegger, see *Being and Time,* 71–75.

the symbols created by our predecessors in the search of truth about human existence? The test of truth, to put it pointedly, will be the lack of originality in the propositions."[3]

A last point of similarity between Heidegger's work and Voegelin's is their emphasis on the intrinsic awareness on the part of consciousness of being something given to itself, something suffered, or "thrown," in Heidegger's terminology.[4] According to Voegelin, consciousness is always at least tacitly, if not focally, aware of not being its own origin, of being a movement in reality that, as Kierkegaard would say, is transparent for the power that established it.[5]

This characteristic, this transparency of consciousness for its origin in something other than itself, is a suitable topic with which to begin a closer examination of Voegelin's theory, since it was his rejection of philosophies that made the subjectivity, the ego-character, of consciousness its ultimate formal structure that prompted the development of that theory, which in its fullness offers an ontology of the human as profound and as dramatically convincing as that of Heidegger.

The Historical Dimension of Consciousness

As he recounts it, it was in 1943 that Voegelin made his first important breakthrough in developing a satisfactory position on consciousness.[6] The occasion was his reading of Edmund Husserl's *Krisis der Europaeischen Wissenschaften* (1936), which he had only recently been able to obtain. He describes what he found there and his reaction to it:

> Husserl elaborated on the motivations of his own work by placing it in the context of a philosophical history. In his conception, the history of man's reason had three phases: (1) a prehistory, of no particular interest

3. "Equivalences of Experience," 122.
4. On Heidegger's "thrownness" (*Geworfenheit*), see *Being and Time,* 174–75, 219–24. For a comment by Voegelin on its meaning in comparison with his own perspective, see "On Debate and Existence," 47.
5. Søren Kierkegaard, *The Sickness unto Death,* 13–14.
6. Voegelin tells the story in *Anamnesis,* chapter 1, "Remembrance of Things Past," 3–13, reprinted in *The Collected Works,* vol. 12, *Published Essays, 1966–1985,* 304–14.

to the philosopher, ending with the Greek foundation of philosophy; (2) a phase beginning with the Greek *Urstiftung*, the primordial foundation of philosophy, that was interrupted by the Christian thinkers but then renewed by Descartes, and reached up to Husserl; and (3) a last phase, beginning with the *apodiktische Anfang*, the "apodictic beginning" set by his own work, and going on forever into the future, within the "horizon of apodictic continuation" of his phenomenology. I still remember the shock when I read this "philosophy of history." I was horrified because I could not help recognizing the all-too-familiar type of phase constructions in which had indulged the Enlightenment philosophes and, after them, Comte, Hegel, and Marx. It was one more of the symbolisms created by apocalyptic-gnostic thinkers, with the purpose of abolishing a "past history" of mankind and letting its "true history" begin with the respective author's own work.[7]

Missing from Husserl's conception of the history of reason was careful reflection on the implications of the fact that present thinking arises from a history that gives it birth and conditions it. He had slighted what might be called the historical dimension of consciousness. This historical dimension is not just the past of human history, "but the permanent presence of the process of reality in which man participates with his conscious existence." Husserl's philosophical triumph, much studied and admired by Voegelin, was his detailed analysis of the intentional operations of the subject, or intersubjective ego. But what he had failed to address in an adequate manner was that those operations are always rooted in a reality beyond themselves, and that awareness of that rootedness is not merely a deduced truth but also an indelible experiential feature of consciousness. "Conscious existence," as Voegelin says, "is an event within reality, and man's consciousness is quite conscious of being constituted by the reality of which it is conscious."[8]

The failure was not Husserl's alone, of course; Voegelin's main concern was how in this respect Husserl's work lay in the mainstream of modern philosophies of consciousness since at least Descartes. Hence he began to conceive a theory that would reintroduce the slighted dimension. The results of his initial grappling with the problems can be found in "On the Theory of Consciousness," the second chapter in the Ameri-

7. *Anamnesis*, 9–10.
8. Ibid., 10, 11.

can edition of *Anamnesis,* originally a letter of 1943 to his close friend and fellow philosopher Alfred Schuetz. The following is a brief exposition of its main points.

"The positive starting point" for an adequate theory of consciousness, Voegelin writes, "is to be found in the phenomenon of attention and the focusing of attention." Attention can be described most simply as a center of energy that is aware and able to focus itself within its horizon of awareness. It can expand or narrow its focus, can intensify or relax its concentration. Its energy is finite and exhaustible, although the amount of strength it commands can perhaps be enhanced through disciplined effort. It does not experience itself as a disconnected moment of awareness, but as a process, with dimensions of past and future. The past and future of this process, however, are not to be confused with the past and future of external things and historical dates; this past and future are "inner dimensions"; they belong intrinsically to the center of energy along with its "present." Finally, as a process with its temporal dimensions, consciousness illumines "from within" the greater, inclusive process of reality in which it shares. It is an illumination within reality, which discloses a horizon of time and meaning.[9]

Though it has the character of a process, and therefore is temporally conditioned, consciousness, Voegelin goes on to argue, is by no means strictly bound by time. On the contrary, "it is the function of human consciousness *not* to flow but rather to constitute the spaceless and timeless world of meaning, sense, and the world's order."[10] What is Voegelin claiming here? Apparently, that while meaning is revealed in experiences intrinsically conditioned by space and time, meaning has a dimension that transcends these conditions. The claim is not so extravagant. If it were not true, there could be no universality to any insight or statement, since no aspect of meaning could transcend the constantly shifting particulars of temporal and spatial differences. Communication would thus be impossible; meaning would be lost in a radical Heraclitean flux. In order for there to be a world of meaning, human awareness must reach beyond the flow of change, or rather *through* the flow of what is changing, to what is not changing; to use Platonic language, through what

9. Ibid., 19–21.
10. Ibid., 16.

"becomes" to what "is." But this "timeless world" of what "is" is nevertheless only apprehended in the matrix of time.

Saint Augustine, in his famous meditation on time in Book Eleven of *Confessions,* concluded similarly that both the past belonging to his memory and the future belonging to his anticipation were species of the present of what is, but the present refracted in the medium of his finite mind. "It is not strictly correct to say that there are three times, past, present, and future. It might be correct to say that there are three times, a present of past things, a present of present things, and a present of future things." But "the present" in itself cannot be said to have any duration, since if it did it would be divisible into past and future; rather, the present is the pure now of attention or awareness that neither was nor will be but is. "[The present] passes so rapidly from the future to the past that its duration is without length. For if its duration were prolonged, it could be divided into past and future. When it is present it has no duration." The human experience of the present, therefore, insofar as it "has no duration," is a kind of transcendence of time. "As for the present, if it were always present and never moved on to become the past, it would not be time but eternity."[11] This mystery of a temporal creature in whose consciousness time is in process of being transcended was for Augustine, as it is for Voegelin, a cause of wonder, but unquestionably a fact.

Voegelin's criticism of Husserl proceeds from this fact. Husserl had held that consciousness was properly conceived of as a temporal stream or flow. But according to Voegelin what flows is not the whole of consciousness but the perceptions, sensations, and images, rooted in the body, that underpin and sustain consciousness. Conscious process receives its character *as process* from its bodily foundations, but it is itself both temporal *and* beyond time. Ongoing transcendence of the temporal is a fundamental given of consciousness; its "present" is created by the intersection of the timeless sphere of meaning with the temporal roots of consciousness in bodily processes.[12]

Explaining to his friend Schuetz the nature of this transcending,

11. Augustine, *Confessions,* 264, 266, 269.

12. *Anamnesis,* 16–17. Though Voegelin does not use the language of "intersection" here, he elsewhere quotes admiringly T. S. Eliot's description in "The Dry Salvages" of consciousness and incarnation as "The point of intersection of the timeless / With time" (*Four Quartets,* 44). See "Immortality," 71, 77.

Voegelin is led to discuss the problem of the relationship between the consciousness that transcends and what it transcends "into." And here we find some statements about mythic and speculative symbols that bring us to one of the gravitational centers of Voegelin's philosophical work: the problems surrounding the experience and knowledge of the oneness of reality from the perspective of human participation.

The temporal world and the realm of meaning that transcends time are both parts of a Whole. But the oneness of reality, we are told, is not given to us as an object of our experience. We do not even have direct experience of the oneness of the various levels of physical being, the inorganic, the vegetative, and the animal. But we do discern that higher levels emerge from and depend upon lower levels; and further, a human being discovers himself or herself as containing all of these, as being an epitome of the full range of the levels of being that exist in the cosmos. "Speaking ontologically, consciousness finds in the order of being of the world no level which it does not also experience as its own foundation." The substantial identity of the physical and conscious levels as one "nature" is therefore an "ontological hypothesis" without which reality would be incoherent. Further, the interdependence of nature bespeaks a common origin, a common "ground," from which things emerge. This "ground," as Voegelin calls it, is also a necessary "ontological hypothesis": "That being which is the ground of all experienceable particular being is an ontological hypothesis without which the experienced reality of the ontic nexus in human existence remains incomprehensible, but it is nowhere a datum in human existence[;] rather it is always strictly transcendence that we can approach only through meditation."[13]

Much shall be said in what follows about Voegelin's notion of the ground. But here it should be noted that the argumentation and language Voegelin uses in describing it in 1943 are very close to Kant's analysis of world (unity of nature) and God (ground of being) as transcendental "Ideas," pure concepts of reason, necessary for the coherence of our understanding of reality and for practical conduct, but not verifiable as objects.[14] For Kant, only that which can be exhibited in sense experience can be considered an object of "experience" and something of which one

13. *Anamnesis*, 27–28, 31, 32.
14. Immanuel Kant, *Critique of Pure Reason*, 236–46.

can claim "objective knowledge"; clearly, something like the "ground of being" would have to remain, for Kant, a pure concept (or "ontological hypothesis"). While the Kantian influence on Voegelin's thinking is obvious, it is significant that Voegelin is noticeably shifting weight here to the experienceable origin of his hypothesis. Notice that he does not say we have no *experience* of the unity of nature or of the ground of being, but no experience of them *as objects*. There are Kantian presuppositions here in the implicit definition of "object" as something conforming to the model of what is given to us in sense-perception, but there is also a clear break from Kant's restriction of "experience" to that which can be incorporated within the conditions of sense-experience. Never in forty years of subsequent work did Voegelin attempt to revise or redefine the basic meanings of "object" or "objective knowing" in a way that would have made them the intentional correlates to experience.[15] But nevertheless, during the course of his career he was increasingly willing to ascribe to experience, if not to "objective experience," involvement with whatever falls within the range of human wonder and concern. Here he speaks already somewhat inconsistently of the ground of being as both a hypothesis and as something "meditatively *experienced.*"[16]

Voegelin here describes the content of such "meditative experience" of the ground only to the extent of saying that at its climax "the intention of consciousness is directed toward the contents of the world, not objectively, through the *cogitata,* but rather nonobjectively toward the transcendent ground of being." Such meditation is, we are told, another aspect of the capacity of consciousness for self-transcendence, directed now toward what is "strictly transcendence." The origin or ground of being is what finite things invite us to recognize by virtue of their existences presupposing it. It is not a finite thing itself, but a Beyond, which finiteness bears witness to, and it "cannot be drawn from that Beyond of finiteness into finiteness itself." Meditative experiences acquaint us with

---

15. Compare the philosophy of Bernard Lonergan, where "object" is defined as that which is intended by a question. For Lonergan, the "to-be-known" intended by a question might be a thing of sense-perception, or it might not. Since what is intended to be known is precisely reality, why not, he asks, let the term *object* correspond to "the real," that is, the full range of reality as intended by the full range of human questions? See Lonergan, *Insight,* 348–84.

16. *Anamnesis,* 29 (emphasis added).

the ground of being in its curious character as a Beyond that we experience *as* a Beyond.[17]

The reference here to a "Beyond" of things is the harbinger of later, increasingly complex and penetrating analyses of what Voegelin eventually came to consider the most important and most misunderstood problem in Western cultural history. His mature work places the experience of strictly transcendent reality at the center of both his theory of consciousness and his philosophy of history. Here Voegelin acknowledges that part of the reason this experience and its centrality are problematic lies in the fact that, while the question about the ground of reality is a common concern of consciousness, a proper understanding and acceptance of the ground as a strictly transcendent Beyond is a rare personal achievement. Nevertheless, we in the West live in a culture informed by that achievement. That is why we tend to dismiss as superstitious or primitive the "mythic" portrayals of the origin of things—that is, representations of ultimate origins in terms of finite beings or events, accessible, in some measure, to human imaginations in our desire for complete explanation. But if, in the West, such myths have been debunked and rendered largely ineffective, and have lost their evocative and consoling power, nevertheless "the spiritualized expressions of the experience of [the ground as] transcendence in intellectual mysticism and philosophical speculation are accessible only to a small minority." The consequence, as Voegelin sees it, is a West that is lost in the cosmos, without "fixed points in the myth." And in this letter to Schuetz, he goes so far as to link the frustrations and paralyses involved in elementary experiences of the ground being unable to find existentially ordering representation to the "orgiastic discharges" of the First and Second World Wars.[18]

Taking Voegelin as one for whom "the spiritualized expressions of the experience of transcendence in intellectual mysticism and philosophical speculation" *are* accessible, we can look to him for an interpretation of consciousness consistent with an understanding of the implications of such experiences. And this we find outlined in this letter, where he describes consciousness as an illuminatory phase or stage in the "unfold-

17. Ibid., 28–29, 32.
18. Ibid., 26.

ing" of a single process of reality. *From a perspective in which the radical transcendence of the ground of being has been distinguished from the actions and processes of the finite world,* the world can be seen as a process of *dynamic emergence from the ground* unfolding in the direction of higher, more complex integrations of finite being: "The differentiation of the experienced levels of being can be made understandable only by interpreting it through the category of process as a series of phases in the unfolding of the identical substance that attains its illumination phase in human consciousness." In other words, consciousness is where reality, or Being, or the Whole of what is, breaks out into awareness and knowledge of itself. It follows—and this brings us to the key issue in Voegelin's brief against Husserl—that the subjectivity of consciousness, the fact that it is "yours" or "mine," is, speaking ontologically, a secondary and derivative phenomenon. Voegelin is explicit about this: "It is doubtful whether consciousness has the form of the I, or whether the I is not rather a phenomenon in the consciousness." "The 'I' seems to me to be no given at all but rather a highly complex symbol for certain perspectives in consciousness."[19]

Now, Husserl had based his attempt to establish an apodictic, scientific philosophy on the supposition that consciousness has no other form or structure than that of the ego: his phenomenological science defines consciousness in general as the "transcendental ego."[20] To Voegelin, Husserl's conception of a transcendental ego was a critical error of the first magnitude, based, he would argue, on two mistakes compounding each other. First of all, Husserl presumed to elevate the notion of the "I" as experienced in its formal position in the nexus of body and world to the status of a pre-experienceable, transcendental consciousness. To Voegelin, this is simply inadmissable. The "I" pertains only to a definite individual, and as such is an ontologically derivative phenomenon—since

19. Ibid., 19, 29. For other and, to some degree, complementary analyses of human consciousness as a stratum in the unfolding of foundationally related but organizationally autonomous levels of being, rising from inorganic through vegetative, animal, and spiritual forms or structures, see Max Scheler, *Man's Place in Nature;* Michael Polanyi and Harry Prosch, *Meaning,* especially chapter 11; and Lonergan, *Insight,* especially chapters 4, 8, and 15. It should be noted that Scheler had an important influence on Voegelin's intellectual development; see Sandoz, *The Voegelinian Revolution,* 53–54, 196n.

20. Edmund Husserl, *Cartesian Meditations,* 18–26.

ultimately consciousness (and ignoring this was Husserl's second mistake) must be said to belong to the timeless ground of time and meaning,
about which we know at least that it is beyond whatever we can know or
designate except through metaphorical or analogical hints and speculations. Husserl, in other words, had marched the claims of a "science" of
consciousness proudly but irresponsibly onto the terrain of mystical and
mythic symbols.

As he concludes his letter, Voegelin expresses an abhorrence of the
supposedly scientific category of the transcendental ego, regarding it as
symptomatic of a modern hubris that rejects the dependence of consciousness on cosmic origins: "The creation of the transcendental I as the
central symbol of philosophy implies the destruction of the cosmic whole
within which philosophizing becomes at all possible."[21] Voegelin makes
his own position clear: human consciousness is always an event within a
historical context of language, community, world, and cosmos, whose
ultimate reference point is a radically transcendent ground of being. Recognition of this full context, as a first principle of any philosophy of
consciousness, makes the notion of an "apodictic beginning" in the modern style of Descartes and Husserl inadmissable. Consciousness is a late
event in the unfolding of the cosmos from its mysterious ground; every
philosopher and philosophy begins, as Voegelin was later to put it, "in
the middle of the story."[22]

Thus the letter to Schuetz of 1943, an especially useful document for
showing how Voegelin's theory of consciousness began to crystallize.
Voegelin's concern with what he judged to be the weaknesses of Husserl's philosophy, notably its ambition to be a definitive "science" of consciousness and its failure to provide orientation with respect to history
and the ground of being, elicited in him a new, convincing clarity about
where to focus his own questions and energies. Adumbrated in the letter
to Schuetz are the basic principles of the philosophical anthropology that
his later writings expand and deepen, and which provide the foundation
for his often virulent criticisms of contemporary culture. Before review-
ing the key points in the letter, however, it should be stressed again that
Voegelin never considered his own theory a novel way of understanding

21. *Anamnesis,* 35.
22. *In Search of Order,* 27.

human nature; to him, its merit lies in its recovery of the traditional insights of philosophers, sages, saints, and prophets.

The most important feature of the letter is Voegelin's insistence that consciousness has the structure not only of an "I" but also of an "other-than-I," since it experiences itself as belonging to the mysterious ground of being. Therefore, the articulation of the meaning of consciousness demands, at some stage, the use of mystical or mythic symbols—that is, symbols that communicate the fact that consciousness participates in a reality whose ultimate meaning transcends human understanding and, in the case of mythical symbols, that suggest an interpretation of that further dimension of meaning consistent with what we do know about reality. Such symbols are important elements not only in a philosopher's account of reality but also in personal and political life, because a human being is not merely a congeries of spatiotemporal processes, but the meeting-place of these with the timeless ground of meaning, and needs emotional and intellectual orientation in that mysterious destiny. Therefore, he concludes that any attempt to explain consciousness in the manner of a science of indubitable propositions trespasses on the mystery of the ground in which consciousness participates.

Consciousness as Participatory Tension

Once it had become clear to Voegelin that an adequate philosophy of consciousness would have to take fully into account the experiences of transcendent mystery that are notably absent, or at best misrepresented, in most of the philosophies of modernity, his work coalesced around an interpretation of consciousness as an illumination in reality and as part of a mysterious story being told by reality. To borrow a distinction from Greek studies, Voegelin's theory wishes to reserve a place in the human search for meaning for both logos and mythos, for rational analyses explaining the functions, procedures, and structures of consciousness—properly theoretical accounts, in other words—but also for appreciations of consciousness as part of a story, a narrative to be told as from the perspective of the encompassing Whole of reality. Voegelin doesn't offer his own story; rather, he directs critical attention to the great philosophical and spiritual mythoi of Western civilization, explaining that what makes a mythos imaginatively compelling is its resonance with what we know to be true about the order of things:

> But how does the listener recognize the story to be true, so that by the recognition of its truth he is forced to reorder his existence? Why should he believe the story to be true rather than consider it somebody's private opinion concerning the order of his preference? To questions of this class only one answer is possible: . . . [it] will have no authority of truth unless it speaks with an authority commonly present in everybody's consciousness . . . [unless it] indeed speaks what is common (*xynon*) to the order of man's existence as a partner in the comprehending reality.[23]

In other words, the ultimate test of the validity of such a mythos is the response it engenders in the consciousness of the listener, and the quality of that response is proportionate to existential maturity and insight. That does not mean, however, that there are no external criteria at all for gauging its merit. An appropriate story of the Whole will communicate to the listener that it is at best a "likely story," an *eikos mythos* in Plato's phrase, and not a definitive account, because the Mystery of the Whole can never be exhaustively plumbed by human insight or creative appreciation. In the modern West, Voegelin laments, we have become accustomed to "stories" of reality and of human participation in it that claim to be, or to be heading toward being, exhaustive explanations. Behind Husserl's representative "apodictic science" of consciousness, there looms the assumption that logos can deliver mythos from all ambiguity. Voegelin's theory of consciousness pulls in the opposite direction of letting its specifically theoretical content take its place within a wider story being told by the mysterious ground of reality; for consciousness and all things "are circumfused by an ambience of mystery that can be understood only in terms of the Myth."[24]

The full-blown conception of consciousness that we find in *Anamnesis* (1966), *The Ecumenic Age* (1974), *In Search of Order* (1987), and various later essays is informed by Voegelin's digestion of an enormous quantity of historical and philosophical materials. His intensive study of the Greek world, and in particular of Plato and Aristotle, especially influ-

---

23. Ibid., 25–26.
24. "The Beginning and the Beyond," 175.

enced its formation. *Anamnesis* contains, among other essays, a seventy-page meditation entitled "What is Political Reality?," which examines the two philosophers' broadest insights into human nature and attempts to rephrase these in a more generalized and self-reflective form as a basis for Voegelin's own theory, a theory that after *Anamnesis* claimed deep roots in the original thinking that opened the Western philosophical horizon. The work of Plato and Aristotle was the original exegesis of consciousness, and it "was essentially successful," in Voegelin's opinion, in clarifying not only the functioning elements of consciousness but also its meaning as a kind of reality that knows its own essence to be participation in the mysterious ordering and creative ground of the cosmos.[25]

Following Aristotle, Voegelin's mature theory describes consciousness as initially a wondering, a questioning restlessness, an awareness of ignorance out of which grows the desire to know. It begins as a "tension" of questioning, the openness of a yearning to know that which is only dimly or partially apprehended. Questioning, of course, reaches its temporary satisfaction in answers. But there is no answer or set of answers that could satisfy once and for all the drive of questioning consciousness, because the range of our questioning easily outstrips the answers available to our finite capacities of knowing. Questioning, as the elementary fact of human consciousness, is not a stage in its growth to be superseded by a stage of unquestioning knowing. However much is known, the desire to know keeps pushing consciousness beyond the horizon of achieved knowledge, and the awareness of ignorance does not diminish, but deepens, as the expanding boundary of what is known expands the boundary of what is known to be not known. The status of consciousness is that of being in-between total ignorance and total knowledge.

Toward the end of *The Ecumenic Age,* Voegelin identifies consciousness with what he calls "the Question" as a means of stressing the ultimacy of questioning in conscious experience: "The Question capitalized is not a question concerning the nature of this or that object in the external world, but a structure inherent to the experience of reality." The Question is the dynamic core of consciousness, what Lonergan calls "the pure question" that ascends from the darkness of the subconscious foundations of existence to reveal the illuminated realm of the manifold intel-

25. *Anamnesis,* 148.

ligibilities of the world of sense and action, and can push onward toward the meditatively ascertained transcendent ground of being, which is revealed in the darkness of its mysteriousness. The direction of that ascent, claims Voegelin, reveals the essential meaning of consciousness: the Question is first and foremost "the quest concerning the mysterious ground of all Being."[26] Since Voegelin knows that most people never explicitly concern themselves with the "ground of Being" at all, one might ask what he means by this assertion.

He means that the desire to know is, generally and comprehensively, a human being's search for the meaning of his or her own existence. But since no one's existence is the cause of itself, the meaning of anyone's existence is ultimately to be found only in the cause of all existence. Therefore, any search for meaning is ipso facto a search for that ultimate cause, whether this fact is recognized or not. In his finest single essay on the Greek discovery of the mind, "Reason: The Classic Experience" (1974), included as a chapter in the American edition of *Anamnesis*, Voegelin presents his interpretation of the Platonic-Aristotelian recognition of this fact:

> Man is not a self-created, autonomous being carrying the origin and meaning of his existence within himself. He is not a divine *causa sui;* from the experience of his life in precarious existence within the limits of birth and death there rather rises the wondering question about the ultimate ground, the *aitia* [cause] or *prote arche* [first beginning], of all reality and specifically his own. The question is inherent in the experience from which it rises; the *zoon noun echon* [living being that possesses intellect] that experiences itself as a living being is at the same time conscious of the questionable character attaching to this status. Man, when he experiences himself as existent, discovers his specific humanity as that of the questioner for the where-from and the where-to, for the ground and the sense of his existence.[27]

Before and after it is anything else, then, consciousness is a questioning whose intention and orientation are determined by its spontaneous, natural goal, the full understanding of its own existence, which is at once

---

26. *The Ecumenic Age,* 317, 320; Lonergan, *Insight,* 9.
27. *Anamnesis,* 92–93. The essay is reprinted in *The Collected Works,* vol. 12, *Published Essays, 1966–1985,* 265–91.

its own origin or ground. The tension between ignorance and knowledge, therefore, is most adequately characterized as a "tension toward the ground."

That "tension of existence," as Voegelin also calls it, is the *fundamentum* of human experience. It embraces the intellectual striving of inquiry; the emotional pulls of love, hope, fear, and despair; and the existential dispositions of trust and anxiety—all the concrete forms in which it is lived. Voegelin relies heavily on certain terms of Plato and Aristotle for his own analysis of the tension of existence, notably the metaphorical *metaxy*, which signifies an in-between status of some kind, and the lamentably untranslatable *noetic* (from the Greek word for intellect, *nous*). We can give some indication of his reasons for that reliance by examining briefly the meaning of the term *nous*.

In the texts of Plato and Aristotle, *nous* refers to the faculty that thinks, that grasps meaning or intelligibility. But it is not only a capacity for apprehending intelligible patterns or structures in reality; it is also the source of order in the soul, the force whose reasoning and judgments allow the soul to resist disordering influences from the surrounding society. Within the context of human action, then, *nous* is conceived as both the power to *apprehend* intelligible order and the force that *creates* intelligible order. Now, in Greek culture, side by side with the emergence of this understanding of *nous,* there unfolded the search, beginning with the Ionians, for a unifying primal element or cause from which to explain the order of the material cosmos. In the course of this search it became clear, eventually, that what was needed was an explanatory principle in the nature of a single, formative intelligence that ordered and moved reality; and in the thought of Anaxagoras one sees for the first time the suggestion that it is *Nous* that guides all things.[28] This is a conception that analogically unites human consciousness, understood as intelligence or reason, with the ground of reality understood as divine ordering intelligence. Thus it is a conception that bridges, at least implicitly, the radical separation between human and divine, mortal and

28. For the texts of Anaxagoras relating to *Nous,* see G. S. Kirk and J. E. Raven, *The Presocratic Philosophers,* 372–75. Voegelin has treated the pre-Socratic emergence of philosophy in *The World of the Polis,* 165–240, where he concentrates, however, on the existential and spiritual advances of Xenophanes, Parmenides, and Heraclitus rather than on the growth of natural philosophy.

immortal. And it is this insight and conception that is carried forward into much more explicit formulation and analysis in the works of Plato and Aristotle, according to Voegelin, in a manner he explains in the following way: "By *nous* [Aristotle] understands both the human capacity for knowing questioning about the ground and also the ground of being itself, which is experienced as the directing mover of questions." And: "In the Platonic-Aristotelian experience . . . man is moved to his search of the ground by the divine ground of which he is in search."[29] What is evident in these encapsulating sentences is that Voegelin insists the synonymous application of *nous* by Plato and Aristotle is to be taken seriously in an ontological sense: the tension of consciousness is not drawn toward the ground as a mere object of possible, or hoped for, knowledge. The ground is consciousness' *own identity;* human consciousness *participates* in the ground; the ground is a Thinking or Intelligence that is the fullness of human thinking and intelligence.

The key word here is *participates.* The use of the concept of participation to indicate the status of something finite in relation to its ontological perfection or fulfillment first appears on the philosophical scene with Plato. Through the Neoplatonists it became a primary category in the thought of the Church Fathers, and it was elaborated by medieval philosophers, especially by Aquinas, into a nuanced principle of metaphysical explanation. Voegelin clearly considers it one of the most important concepts to have emerged from the philosophical explanation of the structure of reality, for he adopts it as his central explanatory term for characterizing the ontological status of consciousness, crediting both Plato and Aristotle with its initial use for that purpose.

Now, the important role played in Plato's thought by *methexis* (participation), *koinonia* (communion), and related terms is well recognized, but Voegelin's crediting here of Aristotle might puzzle the historian of philosophy. In the *Metaphysics,* criticizing Plato's doctrine of Forms, Aristotle sternly dismisses the language of participation as mere "empty words and poetic metaphors." Aristotle the logician recognizes that there is something essentially ambiguous about the concept. But, Voegelin would point out, "the Philosopher" is himself led to use a synonymous

29. *Anamnesis,* 95, 149. See Plato, *Timaeus* 47e–48a, 51e; and Aristotle, *Metaphysics* 1072b14–31, 1074b15–1075a11.

term, *metalepsis* (communion, participation), when attempting to explain how *nous* is related to the intelligibilities it apprehends: "Thought (*nous*) thinks itself through participation (*metalepsis*) in the object of thought (*noeton*); for it becomes the object of thought (*noetos*) through being touched and thought, so that thought (*nous*) and that which is thought (*noeton*) are the same."[30] Voegelin interprets this to mean that the relationship between knower and known, thought and being, is neither a meeting of completely different realities, nor a merging into absolutely identical reality, but something in-between the two: the knower and what is known are, mysteriously, both the same and distinct. That is what participation means, then: a simultaneity of sameness and difference. Voegelin would say that Aristotle, in spite of his criticisms of Plato's use of the notion of participation, doesn't hesitate to use *metalepsis* to explain the relationship between thought and being because he needs a concept that conveys simultaneous sameness and difference. For consciousness is conscious *of* reality and conscious of *being* reality; it is conscious *of* the ground of being and conscious of *being* the ground of being. Human *nous* and divine *Nous* are the same and yet not the same.

With explicit homage to the Platonic-Aristotelian analysis as he interprets it, Voegelin lays down the provocative principle for his own theory: consciousness is not exclusively human. Or rather, what is human about consciousness is precisely that it transcends its mere humanity through conscious participation in the ultimate formative origin of its own existence, its own divine ground. Following a formulation of Plato's, consciousness is something like a divine-human *metaxy*, or in-between. It is an intermediate area of reality, in-between the temporal and the timeless, constituted as a questioning and knowing awareness in-between ignorance and knowledge. It is not a *merging* of the human and divine, but the place of their interplay, where a derived, created being suffers a degree of participatory creativity insofar as it is one with the origin out of which it realizes it has emerged. "The In-Between of existence is . . . the meeting-ground of the human and the divine in a consciousness of their distinction and interpenetration."[31] It must not be thought that Voegelin

---

30. *Metaphysics* 991a20–22; 1072b20ff. The translation of the latter passage is Voegelin's, *The Ecumenic Age,* 190.

31. Voegelin, "On Hegel: A Study in Sorcery," 233.

is attempting to divinize humanity outright. On the contrary, his emphasis is always upon the limitations of human knowledge and power. The
tension toward the ground is *participation,* a type of identity which is also
a non-identity—in Hegelian language, an identity of identity and non-
identity. In order to confirm that such an interpretation of consciousness
is basic to the Western philosophical tradition, Voegelin states,

> [I]t will be sufficient to recall a few equivalent symbolizations of the
> central issue, i.e., the experience of participation and the consequent
> identity and non-identity of the knower with the known. That being
> and thinking are the same, was the insight of Parmenides; that the logos
> of his discourse was the same as the logos of reality expressed by the
> discourse, the insight of Heraclitus. The symbolism of participation, of
> *methexis* or *metalepsis,* is both classic and scholastic. *Aletheia,* with its
> double meaning of truth and reality, is Platonic-Aristotelian. The iden-
> tity and non-identity of the knower with the known has its equivalent in
> Hegel's sophisticated definition of absolute reality as the identity of
> identity and non-identity—though in this case our agreement must be
> qualified because of Hegel's lapse from the analysis of a structure of
> consciousness into the construction of a system.[32]

Objections to participation as a central principle of metaphysical explanation will always be heard, and understandably so: it is an expressly

32. "Equivalences of Experience," 122. It may be thought that Plato himself did
not place the weight on the symbol *metaxy* that Voegelin apparently considers that he
did. Voegelin refers to two passages, one in *Symposium* and one in *Philebus,* where the
symbol plays a prominent role. In the passage in *Symposium,* it is said (by Diotima to
Socrates) that love (*eros*) is a spiritual power (*daimonion*) and, like all of our experiences that may be described as spiritual, is "halfway between (*metaxy*) god and man"
(202e). Specifically, the spiritual *eros* that guides the philosophical search for truth
moves in the in-between realm where mortals and immortal divinity have intercourse
(203a). This is a realm between knowledge and ignorance (*metaxy sophias kai ama-
thias*) (202a), between riches (*poros*) and poverty (*penia*)—and may be characterized,
Voegelin argues, as the properly human sphere of finite imperfection knowingly seeking its greater perfection. In *Philebus,* reality in general is given an ontologico-mathe-
matical description as existence intermediate between (*metaxy*) the One (*hen*) and the
unlimited (*apeiron*) (16c–17a). Voegelin claims that Plato's recognition of his own
consciousness as an in-between kind of reality tending toward the unity of perfection
led him to conceive all of reality in the same fashion: "Once the truth of man's existence had been understood as the In-Between reality of noetic consciousness, the truth
of the process [of reality] as a whole could be restated as the existence of *all* things in
the In-Between of the One and the Apeiron" (*The Ecumenic Age,* 185).

antilogical (or supralogical) concept. It intentionally violates the law of noncontradiction and affirms a *coincidentia oppositorum*. It proclaims that two are really one, and yet remain two. In its philosophical usage, one could say that the notion of participation has both a rational-critical —or, as Voegelin would say, "noetic"—component and a myth-oriented component. It is, first of all, a rational-critical or noetic concept, since the logical categories of identity and non-identity are presupposed in its specification of a distinct kind of ontological relationship, one in which identity and non-identity are judged to hold true *simultaneously*. But at the same time, it functions as a myth-oriented symbol by evoking the prelogical experience of the one-in-togetherness or consubstantiality of all things, the knowledge that all things are identical in the great "stream of being," the Whole. Only the presence of both of these components gives the single word *participation* the ontological precision to satisfy at the same time the demands for both a rational-critical and mythos-sensitive account of consciousness.[33]

With respect to the nonhuman aspect of what he describes as the human-divine participation of consciousness, Voegelin is at pains to explain that such terms as *the divine, the ground,* and so on, are no more than analogical symbols representing the mysterious origin of things. The language of "the divine" is that of refined analogical symbols derived from myth; the language of "the ground" is one of analogical speculative symbols. Both of them convey the understanding that our own origin is something mysteriously "beyond" the range of finite things; their difference lies in the evocation, on the part of the myth-derived language, of an ultimate or ulterior conscious purposiveness. Why does Voegelin, who uses the two types of language interchangeably, feel justified as a philosopher in using the myth-derived language of "the divine"?

He might say that in answering these questions it is again helpful

33. When Voegelin writes of "noetic" discoveries and of "noetic" interpretations, he is referring to the achievements of the Greek philosophers in critically clarifying the structures of understanding and reasoning, and to all interpretations of consciousness and reality that are informed by that critical clarification. "Noetic interpretations arise when consciousness, on whatever occasion, seeks to become explicit to itself. The endeavor of consciousness to interpret its own logos [rational structure] shall be called noetic exegesis" (*Anamnesis,* 148). In what follows, for the sake of clarity, the term *rational-critical* will sometimes be used in a manner parallel to Voegelin's use of "noetic."

to look at the Platonic-Aristotelian breakthroughs. First of all, as we have seen, when the ground first comes into view with the Greeks as a transcendent formative origin, it does so as an ordering Intellect. The language of "the divine" merely reflects analogically our experience of intellect as conscious and purposive. Further, this is not an intellectual discovery that occurs in an affective vacuum, but rather takes place under particular conditions of existential disposition, which Plato has described and dramatized with great poetic power in his dialogues. Plato specifies *philia* and *eros,* especially, as what Voegelin would call the "concrete modes of the tension" in which the ground reveals itself as timeless being beyond cosmic process. A loving openness in the search for truth about the ground, a "joyous willingness to apperceive" as Voegelin at one point describes it, is decidedly a condition for the revelation of its transcendent character.[34] To state the matter fully: the existential precondition for experiencing the meditative insights in which the ground is philosophically disclosed as timeless transcendent being is a loving openness to the goal of the questioning desire to know. But consciousness is participation in, not observation of or confrontation with, the ground. The loving disposition, no less than the understanding of the questioner, is experienced as a manifestation of the ground that initiates and compels the movements of consciousness. The ground that is manifest in the desire to know is not properly symbolized as an indifferent Intelligence, but as the loving wellspring and fulfillment of the *eros* of the search.

Voegelin's emphasis on the participation of human consciousness in its own ground therefore bears crucial implications, as he takes pains to point out, for his conception of "the divine." "The divine," in Voegelin's philosophy, does not refer to a being, or a substance, that can be defined apart from a consideration of the activities of human consciousness. To be sure, "the divine" refers to the transcendent ground of finitude and finite consciousness. But—Voegelin insists—this transcending reality is only encountered in its interpenetration with the temporal conditions of consciousness. Only through the discovery of itself as a tension of questioning engaged in transcending the conditions of finitude is consciousness able to discover "the divine" as a dimension of reality distinct from "the temporal world." Such a discovery is therefore an act of dissociat-

---

34. *Anamnesis,* 97–98; *The Ecumenic Age,* 236.

ing, or differentiating, elements that are indissolubly one in the tension of consciousness. "The divine" and "the world" only become clearly distinct from each other when consciousness, which is somehow both at once, identifies them as the opposing limits of its own nature. Accordingly, Voegelin speaks of them as the "poles" of the tension of consciousness—and, he warns, "the poles of the tension must not be hypostatized into objects independent of the tension in which they are experienced as its poles." Consciousness, in other words, may extrapolate "divine" and "world," "transcendence" and "immanence," by meditating upon and understanding what it itself is—a kind of reality that is both their union and a tension between them—a *metaxy.*[35]

A consequence of this position is that the symbol *human* becomes essentially ambiguous, insofar as it refers both to the creature of finite consciousness who apprehends himself or herself as distinct from the ground of being and to the in-between where transcendent and immanent, "divine" and "world," interpenetrate. Voegelin is very conscious of this ambiguity; perhaps his most successful attempt to clarify it is in this passage from his "Immortality" article:

> When man discovers his existence in tension, he becomes conscious of his consciousness as both the site and the sensorium of participation in the divine ground. As far as consciousness is the site of participation, its reality partakes of both the divine and the human without being wholly the one or the other; as far as it is the sensorium of participation, it is definitely man's own, located in his body in spatio-temporal existence. Consciousness, thus, is both the time pole of the tension (sensorium) and the whole tension including its pole of the timeless (site). Our participation in the divine remains bound to the perspective of man. If the distinction between the two meanings of consciousness be neglected, there arises the danger of derailing into the divinization of man or the humanization of God.[36]

35. *Anamnesis,* 104. Voegelin also defines the terms identifying the "poles" as "linguistic indices." In this connection, Anibal A. Bueno understandably complains that Voegelin tends to speak of the *metaxy* as a locus, whereas he would more consistently identify this term too as an "index," that is, as a symbol that signifies an essentially abstract intelligible relation ("Consciousness, Time, and Transcendence in Eric Voegelin's Philosophy," 106). But see the next section in this chapter, on Voegelin's coming to include *metaxy* in his late-developed category of "reflective symbols."

36. "Immortality," 90.

This double meaning of consciousness, and therefore the ambiguity of the term *human,* is inescapable, in Voegelin's view, because human participation is simultaneously an identity and non-identity with its ground. The centrality of the notion of participation in Voegelin's theory of consciousness, and his desire to protect what he considers to be the ontological truth that its logical ambiguities represent, allow him to be satisfied with a certain ambiguity of meaning in key terms.[37] When he uses the term *consciousness,* Voegelin usually has in mind that tension that ontologically embraces the poles of transcendence and immanence, timelessness and time; when he juxtaposes *divine* and *human,* he intends a distinction between the ground of being in its ultimacy and perfection and the tension of consciousness that merely participates in the transcendence and creativity of that ground. In Voegelin's philosophy, therefore, the terms *divine* and *human* refer not to "beings" or "entities" but to certain orders of relationship that obtain within reality, orders that become apparent when consciousness reaches, as it did first in the classic philosophers, a certain stage in the explication of its own intelligible structure, an explication that reveals that consciousness is "human" precisely as a divine-human encounter.

With his description of human consciousness as divine-human encounter, Voegelin has moved perhaps as far as it is possible to move from the twentieth-century intellectual mainstream. He advises us that if today we are suspicious of such a conception, it is because the philosophical meanings of *God* and *man* can be, and have been, torn loose from their experiential origins in meditative discovery and misconstrued as describing entities, existing in substantive separation from each other after the manner of physical objects, about which anyone with common sense can have a reasonable opinion. If human consciousness is thus considered to be one kind of substance, with God spatially beyond the world as a kind of supersubstance, then the notion of divine-human encounter, and indeed the language of "the divine" itself, will invite skepticism and dismissal. But that will be, in his view, because the philosophical meanings of the words *God* and *man* have been deformed beyond recognition.

37. Voegelin discusses the necessary ambiguity of the symbol *reality* in *Anamnesis,* 163–66.

Reflective Symbols

In 1987, two years after Voegelin's death, a new formulation of the basic principles of his theory of consciousness appeared in the long-awaited fifth and final volume of *Order and History, In Search of Order.* The fundamental insights are the same, but there is a new economy to the explanatory framework, a refinement of distinctions that led him to ac-knowledge it as his master achievement in the area. We have the testi-mony of his widow, Lissy, who writes in the foreword to the volume: "He let me know that he knew very well that these pages are the key to all his other works and that in these pages he has gone as far as he could go in analysis, saying what he wanted to say as clearly as it possibly could be said."[38]

Voegelin's position had always been that a philosophy of conscious-ness must explain it both in terms of the operations and faculties of a subject and in its nature as an event of illumination within the Whole of reality. His last writings continue to address the coexistence of these two interpretive perspectives through the explanation that we may portray consciousness as having two "structural dimensions." On the one hand, consciousness belongs to a subject, and "in relation to this concretely embodied consciousness, reality assumes the position of an object in-tended." Thus "intentionality" is one "dimension" of consciousness, and the wide-ranging and detailed analyses of the conscious intentionality of the subject carried out by Brentano, Husserl, and others represent a major theoretical advance in the understanding of that dimension. But consciousness is also something that occurs within the mysterious Whole. Intentionality as a structure belongs to consciousness as indi-viduated; but that intending is also an event of illumination within real-ity, in which reality discloses its own meaning to itself. Since *Anamne-sis,* Voegelin had consistently used the term *luminosity* to refer to this identity-aspect of the simultaneous identity and non-identity of knower and known, thought and being, and now he names it as a second struc-tural "dimension" of consciousness.[39]

The theoretical precision attained by contrasting intentionality with

38. *In Search of Order,* xv (unnumbered).
39. Ibid., 15–16.

luminosity allows Voegelin to advance in these pages, to some degree, one of the most underdeveloped aspects of his work, the philosophy of language implied by the twofold perspective of his theory. All language, we are told, is both intentional and luminous. That is, all language is referential, pointing to meanings intended by the subject, and to that extent language is properly conceived of as a tool or a conventional "set of signifiers"; while at the same time language is granted by reality and is the medium through which reality is illumined, a fact expressed in Heidegger's famous dictum, "Language is the House of Being."[40] Words and their meanings, as Voegelin says, belong to the story being told by reality as much as to the humans who use them. "Conceptual analysis," as language that aims to make rational-critical sense of the world and the subject knowing it, clearly operates out of a dominating awareness of the intentional dimension of consciousness. But other types of language arise from "listening" to what reality has to say and letting its "story" be told. "Mythic and revelatory symbols" fall into this category, as do, though Voegelin does not mention them here, the many voices of art.[41]

Now, according to Voegelin, Platonic-Aristotelian philosophy includes the explicit recognition that what he now calls intentional concepts—that is, the noetic or rational-critical language of "nature," of form and matter, of elements and causes, of essences, of being and becoming—are complementary to, and do not invalidate, luminous symbols, the language of mythoi. "Aristotle," he asserts, "recognizes both Myth and Philosophy as languages man can equally use to express the truth of reality, even though he accords to Philosophy the rank of the instrument that is better suited to the task."[42] And Plato's dialogues make abundantly clear his understanding that the explanatory successes of logic and dialectic do

40. Martin Heidegger, "Letter on Humanism," 193. For Heidegger this is the over-riding meaning of language to which all notions of it as "signification" must be considered secondary. "In its essence language is not the utterance of an organism; nor is it the expression of a living thing. Nor can it ever be thought in an essentially correct way in terms of its symbolic character, perhaps not even in terms of the character of signification. Language is the lighting-concealing advent of Being itself" ("Letter," 206). Voegelin would see in this viewpoint a dangerous tendency toward letting the intentional, the human, perspective of consciousness and language be imaginally swallowed up in a too-great identification with the luminous (or divine) perspective.
41. *In Search of Order,* 17–21.
42. "Equivalences of Experience," 125.

not eliminate the human need for affective and existential orientation through luminous symbols. If Plato attacked the classical poets because of their misleading representations of the gods and the heroic virtues, and because of the dangerous psychological seductions of dramatic mimesis, he also expressly balanced his logical and dialectical analyses of being and becoming with a score of magnificent myths whose power to move and persuade are more than mere testimony to his poetic genius. Voegelin is emphatic that, far from it being the case that Plato "resorted" to myths when his powers of rational analysis fell short or when he balked at discrediting a sacrosanct topic or tradition, his myths were careful symbolic constructions intended to maintain a circumambient vision of the Whole of such persuasive appeal that the cognitional control over reality achieved by the logical arguments would not have the effect of unbalancing consciousness by obscuring its luminous and mysterious character. Plato, in other words, was sensitive to the problem of the coexistence of the two dimensions of consciousness, and he "coped with it by using both conceptual analysis and mythic symbolization as complementary modes of thought in the quest for truth." And he was able to do so because consciousness has the capacity to be aware of both of these structures and of their coexistence. That is, the two dimensions can, as Voegelin puts it, "move into a reflective distance in relation to a consciousness" that is critically aware of them both.[43]

Assuming such a critical awareness on Plato's part, there is still nothing in his work like a reflective exegesis of the structures of consciousness in the manner of Voegelin's theory of "tension," "poles," "intentionality," and "luminosity." That greater theoretical refinement of analysis, Voegelin would argue, is due to the *third* structural dimension of consciousness beyond its intentionality and luminosity, its reflective distance to itself, becoming sufficiently recognized, explored, and articulated. Plato's writings, Voegelin would say, with their magnificent balance of logos and mythos, speak to us implicitly of his "reflectively distancing remembrance" of both the individual and participatory dimensions of consciousness; but in Plato, the self-analysis of consciousness is not yet so differentiated that reflective distance itself comes into view. Voegelin's specification and analysis of it as a third structure of consciousness is

43. *In Search of Order*, 17, 32.

offered, in *In Search of Order,* as a distinct theoretical advance over both the classical philosophies and also those of modernity insofar as the latter, especially German Idealism, inadequately explain the relation of the reflexive capacities of consciousness, which they explore in detail, to its other structures; and this advance, he maintains, has a retroactive bearing on the proper interpretation of his own earlier work—for he now claims the essentials of his own theory of consciousness to be an analysis in the medium of "reflective symbols."[44]

These distinctions help us to understand just what Voegelin's theory is, in contradistinction to other types of philosophy of consciousness. He himself asks the question, rhetorically, as *In Search of Order* proceeds: are the terms of his own analysis—such as *tension, luminosity,* and so on—to be taken as unambiguous concepts? as evocative luminous symbols? The answer is neither. They belong, he claims, to a third genus of formulation distinct from the other two. The "tension" of participatory consciousness, the "poles" of the tension and its "metaxy," "intentionality" and "luminosity," are neither the hard and fast categories of a definitive logical or scientific account of consciousness, nor mythopoeic symbols providing assistance in spiritual practice but, as Voegelin now calls them, "reflective symbols," heuristic categories that identify, from the perspective of reflective distance, the primitive complex of elements that consciousness encounters when it achieves an adequately differentiated understanding of its own ontological structure.

The Differentiation of Consciousness

Having followed the development of Voegelin's theory to its end, one can appreciate the overall unity of that theory, the consistency with which it unfolds through four decades. Even with their novelties, the ideas and formulations of *Anamnesis, The Ecumenic Age,* and *In Search of Order* are clearly of a piece with the principles suggested in the 1943 letter to Schuetz. The non-subjective dimension of consciousness, its "luminosity,"

44. Ibid., 40–41. On "reflective distance," see also Voegelin, "Wisdom and the Magic of the Extreme: A Meditation," especially 343–45; and "The Meditative Origin of the Philosophical Knowledge of Order," especially 49–51.

has remained the primary focus throughout. Just what consciousness belongs to as a luminous event in reality has been continuously acknowledged to be a mystery beyond human explanation, though the ground of being has solidified, in the course of Voegelin's analysis, from an "ontological hypothesis" into the divine partner in the participatory tension of existence. Our overview of this development and of Voegelin's abiding concern with the fact that consciousness is aware that it belongs to something which can only be said to be beyond whatever world it can know, puts us in a position at last to consider what is probably the most important and certainly the most innovative feature of Voegelin's philosophy: his theory of the differentiation of consciousness.

According to Voegelin, *the* critical event in the history of Western consciousness is its discovery that the divine origin of things is not itself something commensurate with the visible, finite world, but is of a transcendent nature. It is a discovery in which consciousness perforce recognizes itself as the place where a divine Beyond can make itself known and articulate, and this entails what Voegelin has called the "stratification" of consciousness through its self-apprehension as having both a worldly nature and an at least partial share in transcendent reality. This event first occurred in decisive and influential manner in the West in two separate cultures, roughly parallel in time: in Israel and in Hellas. The first three volumes of *Order and History* take their plan from these facts. *Israel and Revelation* traces the shift from the "compact" consciousness of the ancient Near East empires in Mesopotamia and Egypt, which had not yet identified a dimension of reality beyond the rhythmic play of cosmic forces and entities, to the differentiation of the "true God" of Israel (and eventually Christianity), who speaks through Moses and the prophets from beyond all mundane reality. *The World of the Polis* and *Plato and Aristotle* detail the growing discernment of transcendent reality in Hellenic culture as its compact mythic horizon dissolves through the intellectual advances of its poets, philosophers of nature, and mystic-philosophers. In each civilizational arena, the consequences were devastating. Both sets of achievements shattered the authority of the mythopoeic patterns of perception that governed traditional social, political, and religious institutions, and both demanded an imaginal restructuring of reality along lines that could accommodate a correlative revisioning of personal destiny along with the symbolization of a divine origin of

meaning now fled behind radical unknowability. In these first three volumes, Voegelin still uses the terms *Reason* and *Revelation* to identify the
achievements of Greece and Israel, respectively. However, the work on
consciousness that first bore fruit in *Anamnesis* leads him to emphasize more and more the common elements in the two traditions. In *The
Ecumenic Age,* Voegelin drops the terminology of *Reason* and *Revelation*
as language deriving from attempts by Christian theologians to monopo-
lize legitimate insight into the divine partner in the differentiating experiences through relegating the philosophers' theology to the status of brilliant speculative deduction performed by unaided "natural reason." *The
Ecumenic Age* is concerned especially, then, with the complementarity,
and then the differences, between what Voegelin now calls the "noetic"
and "pneumatic" (spiritual) differentiations; and the concentration on
the significance of these achievements so dominates the interpretation of
history that emerges in the work that with it, as John William Corrington
has remarked, the entire multivolume study "has become, explicitly, a
description of the process of differentiating consciousness . . . and in so
doing, has subordinated every other aspect of human experience to that
theory."[45]

The next chapter will examine the differentiating experiences and
their consequences. Here it should be noted only that both the Israelite-
Christian experiences that discern a Creator God so radically beyond all
cosmic processes that He creates them ex nihilo through His "Word,"
and the Greek rational-critical experiences that discern the radical transcendence of the divine, set the stage for the discreditation of earlier
mythic representations of the divine and their "stories" of the Whole.
More important yet, the rational-critical modes of thought derived from
Greek philosophizing have tended toward the discrediting of *all* mythic
expression, even of the refined philosophers' myths of Plato and the spiritualized or pneumatic myths of Judaism and Christianity. The first
explicit challenge to the authority of mythic expression as such appears during the Greek Enlightenment of the sixth to fourth centuries
B.C. The dissolution of that authority can be further traced through the
rational-critical challenge posed to Judaism and Christianity by philoso-

45. "Order and Consciousness/Consciousness and History: The New Program of
Voegelin," 157.

phers insensitive to the nature of "luminous symbols" and finally to the all-out attack on myth in recent centuries arising from passionate commitment to the modern mathematizing sciences as unique arbiters of the true and the real.

Consistent throughout all of Voegelin's work is a concern for our loss of the myth in the West. He associates with it a modern decline in sensitivity to the luminous dimension of consciousness, which means a decline in sensitivity to our being constituted within a cosmic Whole whose mysterious ground has granted to us our very existences. In the following, Voegelin's position on the function of myth will be examined, along with his treatment of mystery—specifically, his delineation of the fundamental mysteries about reality and human nature that come sharply into focus as the result of the parallel differentiations of consciousness.

· 2 ·

THE QUESTION OF THE GROUND

Voegelin's notion of the differentiation of consciousness may be clarified by setting it off against what he considers to be the foundational structure of consciousness that does not change, but rather constitutes the transhistorical basis for its historical transformations. Implicitly rejecting modern and postmodern arguments for a radically historicist view of conscious experience, Voegelin asserts that there are indeed invariant structures in consciousness, the most elementary of which is the "tension" of questioning. Consciousness is in essence the Question itself, arising from wondering ignorance and continuing to press beyond everything that comes to be known. The concrete questions and answers change, but not the dynamism of questioning, nor the incompleteness of its satisfaction. For as explained in the last chapter, the Question, the search for meaning, is for Voegelin at its core a search for the mysterious "where-from and where-to, the ground and sense of existence." Existence is a "tension toward the ground," and it cannot but ask questions about the ground, about the origins of things, about why things are as they are, about what they came from and how they came to be, about what they ultimately mean. If the ways in which such questions are asked and answered vary, nevertheless "the complex of experience-question-answer as a whole is a constant of consciousness."[1]

Voegelin has found it convenient to explain the historical differentia-

1. *The Ecumenic Age,* 75.

41

tions of consciousness in terms of how the question of the ground is asked and answered. In all pre-differentiated cultures, answers to this question take the form of complexes of stories, or myths, which relate the specific actions of divine personages or occurrences during a primordial, sacred time in order to explain the reasons for the present existence of things and for the specific manner of their present existence. In other words, the ground of reality is represented in terms of numerous concrete entities, principally "the gods," which are themselves parts of the Whole of the imaginable realm of the "cosmos." With the intellectual advance of higher civilizations both East and West, such myths are increasingly "rationalized" through the speculative construction of causal chains of explanation, which extrapolate from lesser to higher origins, in many cases leading finally to a single highest divine element or principle in the cosmos. Voegelin calls this mixture of mythic representation and speculative extrapolation "mytho-speculation," describing it as a "transitional form" between, on the one hand, more pure or compact forms of mythic thinking in which there is as yet no rigorous systematization of such causal chains and, on the other hand, later symbolizations of the ground that move beyond cosmic representation altogether. For in selected societies there occurs the insight that no image, no name, and no explanatory concept can adequately express the nature of the ultimate ground of things, because it is absolutely transcendent and so beyond human knowing. Such is the progress of discoveries culminating in what Voegelin calls "the differentiation of consciousness." As consciousness is where knower and known, thought and being, meet and correspond, what "differentiates" is twofold. On the side of being, reality splits into (1) the things of the cosmos and (2) their ultimate origin, which is not another cosmic thing, but somehow beyond all cosmic things. On the side of the thinker, correlative to this bifurcation of reality, human beings discover themselves not only to be things in the sense-perceived cosmos but also to be engaged in transcending it. Consciousness is found to be a Question "that leads to the Beyond of the world because it is not altogether of the world in which it is asked."[2]

2. Ibid., 64; "The Beginning and the Beyond," 176. For a similar analysis of mytho-speculation, from which Voegelin's may be derived, see Henri Frankfort, H. A. Frankfort, John A. Wilson, Thorkild Jacobsen, and William A. Irwin, *The Intellectual Adventure of Ancient Man,* 8–10.

The differentiating break with the cosmos, as Voegelin presents it, can itself be more or less radical; he speaks of "incomplete differentiations" and "tentative breakthroughs," such as those represented by the texts of Confucius, the *Tao Te Ching,* Buddhist teachings, and the Upanishads.[3] The most radical breaks, he claims, occurred in Hellas and Israel, where what he calls the "noetic" and "pneumatic" differentiations respectively led to the unique constellation of discoveries and problems that shaped the foundations of Western culture. Their most striking consequence has been the thoroughness of the dedivinization of the spatiotemporal world in the West, a result of the insights of the two traditions of philosophy and Judeo-Christian spirituality complementing and assisting each other in the removal of the ground to pure transcendence.

In order to appreciate in some measure Voegelin's analysis of the intellectual and existential challenges arising from these events, so that we can appreciate how they make conspicuous the mysteries of human participation in the Whole, we will take a closer look at his account of the pre-differentiated, compact setting of the differentiating experiences, a setting Voegelin attempts to describe through his notion of "the primary experience of the cosmos."

The Primary Experience of the Cosmos

The primary experience of the cosmos may be loosely defined as what is felt and known about reality prior to philosophical or spiritually differ-

3. *The Ecumenic Age,* 285, 321. Gregor Sebba justifiably maintains that "Voegelin has tried hard to do justice to the East, but his heart is not in it" ("Prelude and Variations on the Theme of Eric Voegelin," 44). Still, Voegelin has clearly examined Eastern cultures in the light of his theory of differentiation, and his writings evidence strong, if not profound, familiarity with the great Eastern religions and "philosophies." He has testified to the influence on his thought of an early exposure to the Upanishads, and there are numerous references to the Upanishads in his work; see especially *The Ecumenic Age,* 319–22, and *The World of the Polis,* 18–19, where the "Brahmanic experience of reality" is described in the context of the fuller differentiations of consciousness in Israel and Hellas. For comments on the Buddha and "Buddhist consciousness," see *The World of the Polis,* 1, 18–19, and *The Ecumenic Age,* 328–29. On Confucius and Confucianism, see *Israel and Revelation,* 61–62. And finally there is his examination of early Chinese political symbols in the sixth chapter of *The Ecumenic Age,* "The Chinese Ecumene."

entiated revelations about it. It is the bedrock experience of belonging to
an ordered totality of things, a cosmos, that in its movements, origins,
and meanings is complete within itself. As Voegelin puts it, "The cosmos
of the primary experience . . . is the whole, *to pan,* of an earth below
and a heaven above—of celestial bodies and their movements; of sea-
sonal changes; of fertility rhythms in plant and animal life; of human
life, birth and death; and above all . . . it is a cosmos full of gods." The
last point is essential. What it means in philosophical terms is that the
ground, the purposive origin of things, is perceived or experienced not as
"beyond," but as contained within the spectrum of spatiotemporal existences. Reality is saturated with divine presence, because the very origins
of things are manifest in the cosmos. Divine presence is experienced as
"the gods," manifest entities, encountered in powers, elements, and regularities in the cosmos, through which they reveal themselves and with
which they are more or less convertible. As a result, for the member of
ancient society, nature is never encountered as a neutral, impersonal "It,"
but as a "Thou," alive with purpose and emotion.[4]

It is difficult for us to perform the leap of imagination needed to appreciate the "intracosmic gods" as signifying something other than naive
poetic fancy and superstition, or perhaps a kind of personality-projec-
tion or even wish-fulfillment. We may be helped, Voegelin's analysis suggests, by approaching the ancient compact consciousness from the direction of the question of the ground.

In order to do so, the following distinction should be kept in mind: the
question about the ground of something is not that about its temporal or
mundane "beginnings" (although, in archaic consciousness, these two
questions are not well distinguished). To ask where a tree "comes from"
in terms of vegetative reproduction is not the same as to ask where it
ultimately, primordially "comes from"—that is, what its metaphysical or
divine origins are. The reproductive explanation can—as Aristotle takes
pains to point out—be stretched out ad infinitum with no rational con-
tradiction.[5] But the question of the originary "coming-to-be," the question about the very fact of existence, carries with it an intrinsic rational

---

4. *The Ecumenic Age,* 68; Frankfort et al., *The Intellectual Adventure,* 4–8,
363–64.
5. *Metaphysics* 1071b6–10; *Physics* 206a9–206b1, 208a5–25, 250b11–252b7.

demand for an explanation affirming a first beginning, a primary origin, or a first principle. The meaning of traditional mythic thinking is incomprehensible to us unless we distinguish these two types of question and see the latter of them, that of primal emergence, to imply the terminus of a ground, however that ground may be symbolized. As Voegelin writes in his exegesis of Aristotle's understanding of the issue, "The knowledge that being is not grounded in itself implies the question of the origin, and in this question being is revealed as coming-to-be, albeit not as a coming-to-be in the world of existing things but a coming-to-be from the ground of being." In ancient societies the myths of origins answer the questions about the ground through creation narratives, which must not be confused with stories about mundane events. "Through its time of the narrative, which is not the time of becoming in the world, the myth expresses the coming-to-be from the ground of being."[6] With this distinction between mundane beginnings and primordial beginnings in mind, it is possible to situate compact mythic thinking by stating that it takes place *in the conceptual horizon of an imputation of the Beginning of things to other things represented as in or belonging to the cosmos.*

Voegelin has approached the self-understanding of ancient societies, as he has all others, in terms of the manner in which they explain and symbolize order in reality. The compact myths of Beginnings are ways of telling how things became ordered. The way they do this is to describe the derivation of certain cosmic things—such as humans—from other cosmic things—such as the gods. Since all of reality is, for ancient mythic imagination, contained in the finite cosmos, there can be no means of explaining the derivation or meaning of anything other than through reference to some other finite reality. Therefore there flourish, in ancient mythic society, what might be called cross-referential explanations of reality. Voegelin attempts to clarify how this operates by distinguishing four "partial orders" of reality as making up what he calls the "primordial community of being." These are divine reality, the physical world, social reality, and the individual human being. Although, as he stresses, there is in compact thinking no hard and fast conceptual separation of any of these orders from one another, we can conclude, he argues,

6. *Anamnesis,* 86. For detail on the distinction between the two types of question, see ibid., 83–88, and Voegelin, "In Search of the Ground," 3–5.

from the ancient texts that the pre-differentiated interpretation of reality proceeds by allowing each one of these "areas" to provide an elucidating model for the explanation of the order in each other area. The explanation advances, first of all, from the divine to the other, ultimately derivative, orders. The political realm of an ancient civilization such as that of Babylon or Egypt, for example, may be explained through the use of symbols denoting the divine realm, so that "the geographical order on the earth is the image of the original in the heavens." And the king who rules over that realm may be symbolized as a god, or as a son of god, thereby uniting society with the divine forces from which it derives and which it copies. But the explanation also moves in the opposite direction—since the gods must be understood and symbolized in terms of the features of the physical and social worlds. Thus the gods are represented as kings and consorts, beasts or plants, reflecting political and earthly life; and the heavens themselves may be interpreted as reflecting earth's geography. Voegelin has written copiously on these structures of symbolization, and their details are not our concern. What we wish to make clear is that the use of mutual analogy allows for the expression of an originating meaning of things *within a closed and integrated network of elucidation that does not penetrate beyond the sphere of spatiotemporal imagination.*[7]

There are three features of the primary experience of the cosmos and its methods of symbolization to be especially noted, and they all pertain to the issue of the underlying oneness of reality.

First of all, the pervasive and often bewildering multiplicity of mutually elucidating analogies in mythic thinking grows out of a dominating awareness that all things are essentially one in that they all belong to the one cosmos. This sense of the unity of all substances, of their "consubstantiality" as it has been dubbed by John A. Wilson in a wording Voegelin has adopted, overrides, in the archaic experience, the distinctness and autonomy of entities to a degree that individual substances are regarded as by and large interchangeable. Within such a perspective, as Voegelin observes with a detectable trace of delight, "men can become gods, gods can appear in the form of man, animals are gods, gods can appear in the form of animals, man can appear in the form of animals, plants can start

---

7. *Israel and Revelation*, 1–8, 27; *The Ecumenic Age*, 72–73.

talking, everything can change into everything else."[8] The primary experience is above all the experience of participation, not only of the human in the embracing order of things but also of everything in everything else.

Secondly, however, it is clear that some things participate in existence in a more enduring fashion than other things. "Consubstantiality notwithstanding, there is the experience of separate existence in the stream of being, and the various existences are distinguished by their degrees of durability." Human beings, for example, last longer than many animals or plants, while society continues beyond the lifetimes of individual human beings, and at the far end of the spectrum the gods preceded and will presumably outlast human society and perhaps the world itself. A hierarchy based on degrees of lasting is implicit in the structure of the primary experience of reality, as a result of which, in the explanation of order through intracosmic analogies, certain areas of reality—specifically, the physical universe and the gods—are accorded a "higher rank of representativeness" with respect to the foundations of meaning in the cosmos. Or: in the pre-differentiated representations of the ground, there is a directional factor, based on qualities of lasting, that ascends penultimately to the physical universe and then to divine forces as the ultimate source of order in the cosmos.[9]

Thirdly, and finally, what Voegelin refers to as the "cosmos" of the primary experience was not itself an object of cosmological mythic thought, and it does not represent simply another entity. It is indeed a mythic symbol, but one arising only from philosophical reflection on the primary experience. The Greek *kosmos* means "the ordered Whole of reality," which is rather a recondite concern: the common matrix assumed "behind" the variegated things of experience. The conception *cosmos* thematizes "the background of reality against which all existent things exist," and as such it is an image created by philosophers articulating their "trust in the underlying oneness of reality, its coherence, lastingness, constancy of structure, order, and intelligibility . . ."; it specifies the unifying depth from which all specific things stand out as foreground. Describing it in this fashion, we can identify it as an early, semimythical, and semiphilo-

8. "Theology Confronting World Religions?" 46. On consubstantiality, see Frankfort et al., *The Intellectual Adventure,* 62–69.
9. *Israel and Revelation,* 3; *The Ecumenic Age,* 76.

sophical figuration of the ground that is recognized, in more differentiated consciousness, to be beyond all finite, existing things. In other words, *cosmos,* in Voegelin's use, is a consciously anachronistic but exegetically necessary symbol representing what, for the primary experience of reality, is an originating ground of things as yet known and felt only in, or among, the diverse field of spatiotemporal things.[10]

It should be apparent, now, why Voegelin considers the traditional mythopoeic understanding of the primary experience to be intrinsically unstable and to demand, with a patient but unrelenting inner exigency, the differentiation of consciousness. The destabilizing factor is the latent presence in questioning consciousness of the insight that no spatiotemporal reality provides a sufficiently convincing answer as to the why, the where-from, and the where-to of existing things. The conditions for the insight are provided by the self-discoveries of consciousness. As consciousness comes to understand and thematize its own nature as something spiritually and not materially constituted, as a formative and receptive intelligence (*nous*), for example, or a spirit (*pneuma*) responsive to the invisible urgings of conscience, duty, and grace, the creative and ordering ground comes to be speculatively removed from material creation. The ground of Beginnings recedes from the realm of the finite and palpable, and the latter, the world of things, is increasingly recognized as contingent upon originating powers beyond it.

In order to convey the genuine difficulties and perplexities involved in grasping that the ground is not another cosmic thing, not something perceivable by the senses, and therefore to the undiscerning indistinguishable from nonreality pure and simple, Voegelin in some places describes the ground as "non-existent reality," reserving the term *existence* for spatiotemporally conditioned phenomena. This leads him to define the tension toward the ground as "a tension between existence and non-existence,"

---

10. *The Ecumenic Age,* 72; "Equivalences of Experience," 127; "Immortality," 92. The word *kosmos* attained its meaning as "world order" or "order of reality" only in the early philosophical speculations of pre-Socratics such as Pythagoras, Anaximander, and Heraclitus. Its prephilosophical meaning appears to have been restricted to such phenomena as the "good order" of adornment on a beautiful woman, the "good order" to be found in a well-disciplined arrangement of military troops, or the "right order" of a political community. See Charles H. Kahn, *The Art and Thought of Heraclitus,* 132–33, 312, and Werner Jaeger, *Paideia: The Ideals of Greek Culture,* vol. I, 110.

allowing his intended meaning of "a tension between temporally conditioned existence and the divine fullness of being in which it participates" to be supplemented by the phrase's unavoidable connotation of "a tension between spatiotemporal existence and nothingness." This is not scholarly mischief or obscurantism—though it may be perceived as such —but gentle dialectical craftsmanship responsive to the fact that for Voegelin's readers, as for those first called to move beyond the primary experience of the cosmos, the differentiation of a reality determined by criteria other than the experiences of sense and imagination is an undertaking fraught with perils of misunderstanding. In the ancient societies, that undertaking reaches its goal when it is realized that in the compact symbolizations the divine fullness of the ground, the "everlastingness" of being, is inadequately represented as types of existing things—as the celestial heavens and, more specifically, as "the gods." What shatters the authority of that symbolization is the discovery that "the astrophysical universe must be recognized as too much existent to function as the non-existent ground of reality, and the gods . . . as too little existent to form a realm of intracosmic things." It is a discovery that reveals "the lines along which the cosmological style [of symbolization] will crack until the cosmos dissociates into a dedivinized external world and a world-transcendent God."[11]

But if there is an inherent instability to the cosmological symbolization of reality in the inadequacy of its representation of the ground, there are also factors that render it stable enough to resist, for millennia, the differentiating breakthroughs. First of all, there are the intellectual obstacles, already mentioned, to conceiving the divine ground as beyond all imaginal representation, as ineffable and in some essential way distinct from nature; and these obstacles are bound up with those involved in the discernment and articulation of an interior dimension of the personality—a rational soul (psyche noetike) for the Greeks, a spirit (ruach or pneuma) for the Hebrews and Christians—that functions as the site of participation in divine transcendence. Secondly, it must not be thought that the breakthroughs are only, or even primarily, a matter of ratiocinative distinctions. Equally significant are emotional factors, for the discoveries are burdened with existential implications. In order for human conscious-

11. *The Ecumenic Age*, 77.

ness to make explicit to itself that the divine Beginning lies beyond the field of existing things, it must face directly the anxiety-provoking fact that all such things, itself included, are merely contingent and not necessary realities—that things might just as well have not existed, or be different from the way that they are. There is a tacit awareness of the contingency of things in pre-differentiated consciousness, of course, but it is not conceptually thematized; it is grasped, rather, as the fragility of a social or natural order threatened, through the passing of time and the turmoil of events, or through the displeasure or perhaps forgetfulness of the gods, with alienation from the sources of power and being, or with destruction through mismanagement or sheer inscrutable divine decree. In other words, the ancient mind too is aware, in a fashion, of the possibility that what is might not have been, of "the mystery of existence over the abyss of non-existence," but this awareness is not yet a clear recognition.[12] And as long as the necessary ground of being is conceived in terms of spatiotemporal entities and events, allowing the time and events of everyday life to be followed by the imagination to where they seamlessly merge with depictions of the primordial, sacred events that explain their meaning and lend them the sanction of necessity, then explicit recognition of the mystery of contingency—the sheer mystery that things *happen* to be—and its attendant anxiety will be avoided.

The Experience of the Beyond

Voegelin's complex and voluminous treatment of the discovery of transcendent reality in the West is one of his richest achievements, the cornerstone of his philosophy of history and one of the most intellectually challenging areas of his work. Certainly, his interpretations of Israelite history, Christian revelation, and Greek philosophy are not free from controversy; while his erudition and philosophical brilliance are generally credited, scholars, especially theologians, with backgrounds of specialized expertise and with less ecumenical interests, have taken issue with some of his major conclusions.[13] As already pointed out, Voegelin's position is

12. Ibid., 72.
13. A survey of the critical literature on Voegelin's religious and political interpreta-

that there are distinct Israelite and Hellenic discoveries of transcendence and that these complement rather than contradict each other. The manner and extent of that complementarity he considers to be almost universally unrecognized—an oversight due, he would say, primarily to the Greek philosophical achievements not being commonly understood as having their roots in experiences of the transcendence of the ground of reality at all. While the experiences of Abraham, Moses, and the prophets of Israel, including Jesus, clearly announce the revelation of a personal God beyond space and time, the Greek interpretation of reality as "Being" has yielded a conceptual vocabulary that is much more ambiguous with respect to its experiential origins. Voegelin would argue, however, that it is impossible to make sense of the writings of philosophers such as Xenophanes, Parmenides, Heraclitus, and Plato except on the assumption that their works represent an increasingly nuanced discernment of an "ultimate realissimum" beyond the world of engendered and perishing things, and beyond too the boundaries of the soul's range of knowledge and participation. And it is the complementary nature of the Hellenic and Israelite breakthroughs that, he would argue further, made classical philosophy the analytical instrument par excellence for the exposition and clarification of meaning in Judaic and Christian spiritual teachings and documents.[14]

This is not the place, however, to pursue questions about the convincingness of his exegeses of historical events or individual thinkers such as Plato and St. Paul, because the historical unfolding of the discoveries of transcendence is of relevance to this study only insofar as it provides the

---

tions can be found in John Kirby, "On Reading Eric Voegelin: A Note on the Critical Literature." A challenge to aspects of Voegelin's interpretation of the Old Testament can be found in Bernhard W. Anderson, "Politics and the Transcendent: Voegelin's Philosophical and Theological Exposition of the Old Testament in the Context of the Ancient Near East"; for criticisms of his interpretation of the Gospels and Christian existence, see, for example, Bruce Douglass, "A Diminished Gospel: A Critique of Voegelin's Interpretation of Christianity"; Gerhart Niemeyer, "Eric Voegelin's Philosophy and the Drama of Mankind"; and Thomas J. J. Altizer, "A New History and a New but Ancient God? Voegelin's *The Ecumenic Age.*" A thoughtful criticism of some aspects of Voegelin's interpretation of Plato and Aristotle may be found in George Anastaplo, "On How Eric Voegelin Has Read Plato and Aristotle."

14. On the Greek discovery of transcendence, see *The World of the Polis*, 207-11, 220-21, 239-40; *Anamnesis*, 77-81; and *The New Science of Politics*, 64-70. On the complementarity of the Greek discovery with Hebrew and Christian insights into transcendence, see Voegelin, "The Gospel and Culture," 173-92.

backdrop for Voegelin's analysis of the nature of differentiation itself. Voegelin's philosophy of consciousness as laid out in his major works does tell the story of its historical development from more compact to more differentiated capacities and states, but it does so in order to provide a coherent and compelling account of the structure of your consciousness and mine, which must cope with the same growth from pre-differentiated to differentiated self-interpretations, through adequate insights into experiences of transcendence, as was undergone in the drawn-out cultural evolution of our collective tradition. According to Voegelin, because the ground of reality *was* discovered by Israelites and Greeks to be something other than its cosmic effects or contents, something beyond the cosmos, the language and images through which we make sense of reality in the contemporary West are dominated by symbols that derive from the differentiated perspectives. But this does not mean that we understand these concepts and images correctly, that we have achieved successful self-appropriation of our own consciousnesses as differentiated. For this is not an easy task. Reality is, for every human being, initially and overwhelmingly the cosmos of the primary experience, into which we are born and which even the relatively rare achievements of articulate experiences of transcendence do not annul but supplement. With a tone of admonishment for those whose intellectual or spiritual sophistication might seduce them into forgetting it, Voegelin emphasizes that the primary experience of the cosmos in which the divine presence of the ground is compactly experienced always remains the *condition* within which the differentiation of a divine Beyond, and of a *nous* or spirit in human existence, takes place. "The differentiation of existential truth does not abolish the cosmos in which the event occurs." "Compactness and differentiation [are not] simply historical stages of consciousness, the one succeeding the other in time, but poles of a tensional process in which the revelation of the Beyond has to overcome progressively a hard core of compact resistance without ever dissolving it completely."[15]

Now, with respect to the question of the ground, the essence of differentiation is the bifurcation of the cosmos into a natural or immanent world and a deeper stratum of reality known solely through consciousness' finding a Beyond to its own (and thus to all finite) nature. The pre-

---

15. *The Ecumenic Age*, 8–9; *In Search of Order*, 99.

vious chapter has already touched on the metaphorical nature of Voegelin's category of the Beyond, and now this point must be amplified.

The reality that transcends the world does not exist in such a way that one might perhaps catch a glimpse of it through an extremely powerful telescope. The Beyond is not something on the other side of a spatial dividing line. When through searching and passion and insight the extraordinary souls of Israel and Hellas discerned a world-transcendent reality, whether it was the true God of Israel, or Parmenides' Being that is other than the world known by sense experience, or the Platonic-Aristotelian *Nous*, what they found (or what was revealed to them) was immediately present *only in consciousness.* The data that forms the "material" for the insight that the finite cosmos has as its ground a reality that is other than finite being is the "movement of the soul," as Voegelin puts it, that discovers its own nature both to presuppose and to be co-constituted by a spiritual reality unrestricted by finite limitations. Unless consciousness finds itself engaged in the questioning tension that so desires to identify the true ground of reality that it finds all the splendors of the cosmos still not enough to explain and satisfy its own restless capacity to think and feel *beyond* those splendors, then there can be no occasion for an epiphany of transcendence. When such a movement does occur, what has happened, in Voegelin's terms, is that the tension of consciousness toward a reality beyond all cosmic contents has become transparent for its own nature as "spiritual," i.e., as related by participation to a ground that is incommensurate with limitation. Of course such a ground is known only in the interiority of meditation and reflection, and so it is nothing in the world that can be pointed to. "Such terms as *immanent* and *transcendent, external* and *internal, this world* and *the other world,* and so forth, do not denote objects or their properties. . . . The terms are exegetic, not descriptive."[16]

To put it another way, the differentiation of consciousness does not entail the discovery of another world. There is only the one cosmos. The "truth of existence," as Voegelin calls human living informed by the differentiating insights that reveal it to be a tension toward transcendence, does not annul the "truth of the cosmos," human living as part of and subject to the rhythms, structures, and laws of finite real-

16. Voegelin, "The Beginning and the Beyond," 185.

ity.[17] On the contrary, the Beyond of finite things can only be manifest *through* finite reality. It would be in line with Voegelin's thought to say that transcendence is a further *dimension of meaning* that is revealed when the finite cosmos is recognized to be inadequate as the source of its own meaning. That is, we become aware of strictly transcendent being when we recognize that finite meaning presupposes an ultimate ground of meaning that can only be non-finite. But while our questioning leads us to recognize this non-finite ground, we also recognize it to lie beyond the scope of our finite imagination and understanding. Thus the restricted dimensions of meaning we understand lead us to acknowledge an unrestricted dimension of meaning that we understand to lie beyond our understanding.

The culturally diverse, concrete symbolizations of a transcendent reality always refer, therefore, to a specific range of experiences intrinsic to consciousness, experiences that "pertain directly only to man's consciousness of his existential tension." But—and this is crucial—the "differentiation of consciousness indirectly affect[s] the image of reality as a whole." How? Most importantly, by draining the physical world of sacrality. The physical universe, originally a cosmos alive with the mysterious powers of the gods, becomes, with the flight of the divine to transcendence, an impersonal "world" or "nature"— either the mundane world created by the world-transcendent God of Israelites, Jews, and Christians, or the philosophically disclosed world of nature consisting of an autonomous network of intelligible structures. With devastating thoroughness, the "truth of revelation and philosophy has become fatal to the intracosmic gods."[18]

But if in the new dispensation no finite thing or set of things can adequately represent the ground, still consciousness, as the site of participation in transcendence, can do so, within limits. Out of the discoveries of transcendence, then, there flows the development of symbols that stand at once for both the true nature of the divine and the true nature of consciousness as the site of participation in transcendence. In the Greek orbit, the central symbol for this divine-human reality is, as we have seen, *nous,* usually translated "intellect" or "reason"; while in Israel and in

17. On the phrases "truth of the cosmos" and "truth of existence," see *The Ecumenic Age,* 8–9, 71–73, 315.

18. *The Ecumenic Age,* 8. For clarification about the relation of "cosmos" to "world," see *Anamnesis,* 78–79; and "In Search of the Ground," 12–13.

Christian culture it is *ruach* (the Hebrew term) or *pneuma* (its Greek translation), usually translated "spirit." While the symbol *pneuma* may not be said to be synonymous with the symbol *nous,* they are functionally equivalent insofar as they both indicate the site where transcendent divine and human consciousness enjoy the intimacy of participation.[19]

Voegelin's interpretation of the degree of equivalence between these two terms, and the specific characters of the distinct experiences to which they refer, is one of the more intriguing aspects of his work. To put his conclusions very simply, one might say that the respective terms differ with respect to the "location" in consciousness that they emphasize: the "noetic experience" centers in the area where questioning, reasoning, and judging perform their operations, whereas the "pneumatic experience," as a "divine irruption which constitutes [a] new existential consciousness," takes place at the axial depth of the personality out of which reason and its structures arise. In the noetic experience, as Eugene Webb has summarized it, "focal awareness . . . is directed to the Nous, the questioning consciousness, while the pneumatic center, that level of reality in the depths of the soul at which it is experientially united with being itself, remains in comparative obscurity." Thus the philosophers are led

19. The Greek philosophers, Voegelin explains, had to develop "a host of new symbols that [expressed] the experience of an area of reality intermediate between God and man" ("Immortality," 89). *Nous* became the divine-human organ that orders reality and apperceives its structure; *logos* the structure itself in both thought and reality; and *psyche* the site where human and divine *nous* reach into and interpenetrate each other in the realization of *logos* (See *Anamnesis,* 91–97; and *The World of the Polis,* 227–39, 292–94). The development of symbols corresponding to these in the Israelite orbit, Voegelin tells us, was hindered by obstacles deriving from the deeply rooted ban on conceiving the human as in any way commensurate with divinity or immortality. The notion of a soul's personal destiny in relation with the divine ground is absent from Israelite culture; the spirit of God (the *ruach* of Yahweh) "is present with the community and with individuals in their capacity as representatives of the community, but it is not present as the ordering force in the soul of every man" (*Israel and Revelation,* 240). Therefore, the symbol *ruach,* designating the stratum of differentiated divine presence in consciousness, did not come to express a mutual participation of human and divine in the individual soul until late in the pre-Christian period. But by the time of Jesus the ban had in effect broken down. His followers used the Greek translation of *ruach, pneuma,* along with the philosophical terms *nous* and *logos,* to communicate their experiences of an "extraordinary divine irruption" in the person of Jesus, and its meaning for every person's opportunity to participate in the eternal life of the spirit ("The Gospel and Culture," 192).

to explore the structure of questioning consciousness itself, as well as the structure of reality that "becomes luminous through the noetic theophany"; while exegetes of the pneumatic experience such as St. Paul concentrate upon "the intensely articulate experience of loving-divine action" at work in the unplumbed depths of the soul. To put this in terms of Voegelin's theory of consciousness, the essential difference between the two experiences lies in which pole, human or divine, is emphasized in the divine-human encounter: the questioning human partner who, desiring to know the ground, finds it to be the Intelligence at the heart of all questioning; or the divine partner, the God whose gracious invasion of the soul turns it toward its truth. In both experiences, however, there is "the same consciousness of existence in an In-Between of human-divine participation, and the same experience of divine reality as the center of action in the movement [of the soul] from question to answer."[20]

It is perhaps more obvious now why Voegelin raises the symbol of *metaxy* to a position of singular importance in his philosophy. It conveys in his view the signal truth about consciousness insisted upon by both differentiations: that the truly human is the "human-divine" sphere "in-between" the cosmic things and their transcendent ground; that this in-between, established through questioning, is a tension *from* the finite *toward* the ground; and that this is the one and only place where the true nature of the divine can, within limits, reveal itself in this world, most glaringly and expressly through the deeds and words of prophets, philosophers, and saints.

It is time, now, to again draw attention to the fact that there is a profound irony at the heart of the differentiating process. It is that as the true nature of the ground comes to be known as something radically distinct from earth and sun, king and Pharaoh, so its hiddenness, its genuine unknowability, is revealed. The human beings who find in their own finite intellectual and spiritual capacities clues to the divine being do so only by recognizing that such being transcends incomprehensibly all manner of being with which they are familiar. To know of a Beyond is to acknowledge something beyond knowledge, to discover a mystery—the basic, primal mystery of the originating ground of all reality.

20. *The Ecumenic Age,* 246; "The Gospel and Culture," 189, 192; Webb, "Eric Voegelin's Theory of Revelation," 105.

This is not to say that pre-differentiated consciousness was not acquainted in its own way with the Mystery. The ancient texts show a deep respect for the inscrutability and occasional unpredictability of the sacred powers that guide the events of the cosmos. But theirs is still a tacit, not a focal, awareness that a strictly unknowable reality lies behind all explanation of origins. It is only when divine transcendence is differentiated to the point where all intracosmic symbolizations of the ground begin to be seen as "false gods," as imaginative fabrications, because their figurations inadequately symbolize a ground known to be other than all cosmic contents, that the mystery of the ground at last comes into focus in all the fullness of its disturbing nature.

Voegelin is perhaps unrivaled in his ability to recount and celebrate the advances in knowledge achieved through the Greek and Judeo-Christian discoveries while simultaneously explaining the cognitive and existential difficulties deriving from the disappearance of the ground into transcendence. His concern to maintain a balanced appreciation of these factors leads him, in his many discussions of Plato, to emphasize that as the latter's exegeses of soul, society, and cosmos unfold their remarkable tapestry of insight, they are studded with references to a ground of reality utterly beyond our possible ken, such as the Agathon in *Republic* whose content is impossible to describe and which can only be referred to paradoxically as "being beyond being" (*epekeina tes ousias*), or *Phaedrus*'s "superheavenly region" (*hyperouranios topos*) from whence all truth and reality are nourished but which has never been and never will be worthily praised by any mortal. Similarly, Voegelin's account of Israelite and Christian experiences describes a continuity, stretching from the Mosaic epiphanies to Jesus' comprehension of his own meaning, of increasingly profound revelations of the "Unknown God" (*agnostos theos*) who is so recondite in terms of time and place that he can be, as taught by the followers of Jesus, the source of inner illumination in every human soul. The philosopher's way of truth and the prophetic call to conversion illuminate existence at the cost of rendering its background an abyss of mystery. As Voegelin puts it, the truly divine ground is known only "against the background of his unknowability."[21] On a few occasions, Voegelin has suggested that Aquinas's treatment of the proper

21. *The Ecumenic Age,* 8.

names of God in the *Summa Theologica* is an exemplary expression of
how both the philosophical and Judeo-Christian differentiations, in complementary fashion, disclose the true nature of the ground only through
simultaneously disclosing its unapproachable mystery:

> In his discussion of Pseudo-Dionysius's *De divinis nominibus,* Thomas
> Aquinas has brought the problem of the depth of the ground to the
> following formulation: The name HE WHO IS is most proper for God
> because it goes beyond the particular forms of mundane life. Beyond
> that name, there is the name GOD, because it signifies the divine
> character of the ground; and beyond that there is the name Tetra-
> grammaton [YHWH], since it expressed the incommunicability of the
> divine substance. (*ST* I, XIII, 11) Thus Thomas identifies three areas
> that we also have encountered in our analysis of the existential tension
> toward the ground: (*a*) the area of noetic exegesis that cannot go
> beyond the symbol of the ground of being; (*b*) the area of the compre-
> hensive pneumatic reality of knowledge to which belongs also the
> experience of being personally addressed by God; and (*c*) the area of
> the incomprehensible, of which we know only that it is the area which
> we touch by the symbolic terms of noetic and pneumatic experiences.
> Insofar, however, as we know about the ineffable beyond the expres-
> sions of experience by means of such symbols as the Ineffable or the
> Silence, this knowledge, too, belongs to the consciousness of the ground
> as one of the dimensions of its logos.[22]

A digression may be permitted here to point out that, in Western civilization, the Jewish, Christian, and Islamic mystical traditions represent
the full flowering of an appreciation of divine mystery, traditions with
which Voegelin is certainly familiar but which he has very rarely mentioned in his writings. For a philosopher so deeply concerned with what
can loosely be called mystical experience, whose writings are specifically
concerned with the concrete historical experiences underlying influential
ideas, and who has even accepted for himself the designation of "mystic-

---

22. *Anamnesis,* 198. On Platonic symbols of transcendence, see *Plato and Aristotle,* 112–17; *The Ecumenic Age,* 228–34; "The Gospel and Culture," 208–9; "Wisdom," 360–62; and "The Beginning and the Beyond," 212–17. For the full passages
under discussion, see Plato, *Republic* 506d–509e, and *Phaedrus* 246a–250c. On the
prophetic revelations of the "Unknown God" culminating in the epiphany of Christ,
see *Israel and Revelation,* 402–14; and "The Gospel and Culture," 194–202.

philosopher," such reticence seems odd.[23] One explanation for it, perhaps, lies in the fact that his primary concern has always remained diagnosis of the roots and consequences of political disorder, especially with
regard to the modern West. The great mystics of various religious traditions are no doubt for him paradigms of the well-ordered, pneumatically
differentiated soul; indeed, he has declared that "classical noesis and
mysticism are the two predogmatic realities of knowledge in which the
logos of consciousness was differentiated in a paradigmatic way."[24] But
the insights of the great mystics are not directly relevant to his major
political concerns, and so they remain offstage in his works—as befits
their emphasis upon silence.

There is another explanation as well for Voegelin's exclusion of the
mystical "traditions" from his exegeses. It is indicated by the word *predogmatic* in the sentence quoted above. In these matters, Voegelin is
seeking above all to communicate an understanding of *original* experiences of pneumatic or noetic differentiation—those of the primary dis-
coverers or those of any of us who follow in their steps—precisely in
order to shake our interest in the fixed verbal formulas or images that
belong to distinct "traditions" that have hardened into competing dog-
mas, and thereby in his view threaten to occlude entirely the commonly
human, transcultural structures of mystical experience. For to Voegelin,
differentiation is by definition a mystical experience. It is clear from
scattered remarks that he considers the mystical side of Christianity to
be the living core of its tradition, and one can easily extrapolate to say

23. Webb, *Eric Voegelin*, 44 n. 43. Voegelin has made various references to such
mystics as Plotinus, Pseudo-Dionysius Areopagitica, the unknown author of *The
Cloud of Unknowing*, Shankara, Meister Eckhart and Jean Bodin, and to such texts
as Rudolf Otto's *Mysticism East and West*, but he nowhere discusses them at any
length. His most extensive comments on the topic of mysticism are in *Anamnesis*,
194–99, where he identifies Jean Bodin and Henri Bergson as modern mystics of an
exemplary stature. As to Voegelin's own mysticism, John Kirby, in "On Reading Eric
Voegelin," states accurately that "if the mystical element in Voegelin's speculations
were treated seriously, one might see the road, not overly travelled nowadays, that
points back to Plato by way of Schelling and Eckhart, as well as Bodin, Scotus
Eriugena, Pseudo-Dionysius, St. Augustine, and Plotinus" (54). Nieli, in "Eric
Voegelin's Evolving Ideas," 97–101, treats briefly what he calls Voegelin's "Platonic-
Christian style of mysticism," and he describes how Voegelin's interest in mysticism,
though certainly deepening in later years, is evidenced in even his earliest writings.
24. *Anamnesis*, 192.

that for him mysticism would constitute the heart of every differentiated religious tradition. Further, one can say that for Voegelin the mystic's experience, defined in broadest terms as the personal, reasonably articulate discernment of or encounter with the ground as transcendent, is the core of what its Greek originators meant by "philosophy" as well. This position is unmistakable in his analysis of the pre-Socratics and of Plato. And this means that, if one is to live the "truth of existence," one must become able to share, to some degree, directly or sympathetically, in the common element of all mystical experience, and this is the apprehension of transcendent being. Consequently, his concern is to acquaint the reader with the experiences that initiate traditions more than with the traditions themselves.

Voegelin's writings return with steady regularity to an emphasis on the need for a certain existential disposition as the precondition for suffering the differentiating experiences. Indispensable is trust in the intelligibility and goodness of reality. Such trust he considers to be the very essence of consciousness, which, as the desire to know, must always be pushing ahead of its present understanding. Questioning is de facto oriented toward what is as yet unknown; and the growth of consciousness toward its implicit goal, which is the complete fulfillment of knowing and loving, comes only by way of approaching the surmised unknown through such attitudes as hope and faith and love. Though this is true of consciousness at all times, a heightened and explicit dependence on hope, faith, and love—the "virtues of existential tension" as Voegelin calls them—is required if consciousness is to suffer the understanding that its very identity is constituted by that which it knows cannot be humanly known with exhaustive adequacy. According to Voegelin, the philosophers' self-exegeses—particularly those of Heraclitus, Plato, and Aristotle—are impressively clear about this existential context for their differentiating experiences: "Reason [or *nous*] is differentiated as a structure in reality from the experiences of faith and trust (*pistis*) in the divinely ordered cosmos, and of the love (*philia, eros*) for the divine source of order." Likewise the classic Christian expression, in the Pauline letters, for the essence of one's relationship to the God of the fathers and of Jesus stresses hope, faith, and love (or charity, *agape*), since our transcendent meaning and destiny as revealed by the Unknown God through Jesus cannot be "seen." In both cultural orbits, Voegelin maintains, the great articulators of the truths of the new dispensation are eloquent and un-equivocal on the issue of the basic "mode of the tension" out of which consciousness may discover its real self: it is that which Voegelin, follow-ing Henri Bergson, calls the "openness of the soul," the trusting desire to participate more fully in the structure of reality, however mysterious. Anyone who would genuinely entertain the differentiating insights and, furthermore, attempt to live in their light must therefore be prepared, Voegelin argues, for "the heroic adventure of the soul" that doing so requires. Many, or most, are not equal to the challenge, for reasons that most often reduce themselves to one: "the very lightness of this fabric" of existence based on faith in a transcendent reality proves "too heavy a burden for men who lust for massively possessive experience." It is *the desire for certainty,* overriding with familiar consistency the desire to know, with its unanswerable questions and its increasing awareness of mystery, that tends to prevent those of us who live in the noetic and pneumatic dispensations from understanding and sharing in the "truth of existence."[25]

And yet for us in the contemporary West, in Voegelin's estimation, there is no alternative to achieving a personal understanding of our own consciousnesses as engaged in a movement toward transcendent reality other than to suffer a kind of existential deformation. The reason for this is that, as already noted, we live in a linguistic and cultural horizon predicated upon the differentiating insights. For example, the "modern scientific worldview" that dominates our contemporary imagination and conception of reality, and that derives proximally from the stupendous theoretical and practical achievements of the modern mathematizing sci-ences, is, ultimately, the legacy of the Greek philosophers' interpretation of reality as a dependably stable configuration of interrelated forms (or intelligible structures) that can be explored and articulated through a variety of discrete but systematically and hierarchically related sciences. This interpretation or outlook is so much the currency of our spon-taneous habits of perception that it takes a good deal of effort to become critically conscious that it is not simply the way reality "looks" when one takes a good look at it, but a specific framework tied to certain assump-

25. "Equivalences of Experience," 122; *Anamnesis,* 97–98; *The New Science of Politics,* 122–23. Bergson's notion of "the open soul" (*l'âme ouverte*) is discussed in his *Two Sources of Morality and Religion,* 37–38, 52–66.

tions and implications. One such assumption is that reality, or being, is completely intelligible. Or, to spell it out: what is real is what is verifiable, and what is verifiable is intelligible; whereas the intelligible cannot be verified, and so cannot be confirmed as real.[26] Though this assumption provides their speculative underpinning, it is not directly relevant to the empirical procedures of the natural or human sciences, and it therefore plays little role in the professional scientific imagination or those influenced by it; nevertheless it does not seem, once articulated, a particularly surprising assertion to the modern scientific mind. A related implication, however, which seems to the modern mind at the very least odd, is that this same interpretation of reality as an autonomous network of intelligible structures is itself unintelligible apart from the assumption of a divine Intelligence. As we saw in the last chapter, Intelligence, or divine *Nous,* is the Platonic-Aristotelian conception of the ground that corresponds to the differentiating insights of the Greek thinkers who made "science" possible. The cosmos is revealed to consist of intelligible structure or form only when the divine ground, compactly encountered in the physical environment, is distinguished from nature and its entities, leaving them stable and predictable (that is, lacking the volitions and volatility of "the gods"). When, as in the contemporary West, we retain the philosophical-scientific perspective of reality as a hierarchically layered system of regular structures and dependable relations and occurrences, and at the same time abandon the associated insight into the ground as transcendent Intelligence, we sever the philosophical image of reality from its root and render nonsensical the "scientific" remainder. As Voegelin sums up the issue:

> Structure as the face of reality becomes historically visible when the polymorphous aetiology of the divine in the myth gives way to the philosophers' aetiology of the divine as the *prote arche* of all reality, as it is eminently experienced in man's tension toward the ground of his existence. Cognitively structured reality, unencumbered by compact experiences and symbolizations of divine presence, is correlative to the theophany of the Nous; the openness toward reality at large depends

26. For a full articulation of this philosophical position both with respect to modern science and to human understanding in general, see Lonergan, *Insight,* especially chapters 1, 9, 12, and 19.

on the openness of the psyche toward the divine ground. No science as the systematic exploration of structure in reality is possible, unless the world is intelligible; and the world is intelligible in relation to a psyche that has become luminous for the order of reality through the revelation of the one, divine ground of all being as the Nous.[27]

Voegelin is under no illusions about the capacity of most, philosophers and scientists included, to grasp what he is saying here, not merely because of the inherent difficulty of the philosophers' insight, but also because in the modern West we have become accustomed to the question of the ground being answered in terms of one or another *type of structure* revealed within the hierarchy of intelligible spatiotemporal structures. In other words, the mundane stratum of philosophically differentiated reality, massively present in language symbols, has come to be interpreted as the whole of reality by latter-day compact imagination and understanding, with the result that the ground is "misplaced somewhere in an immanent hierarchy of being." Our culture is, in Voegelin's view, overwhelmingly influenced by speculative interpretations of reality performed by consciousnesses that have not sufficiently grasped the meaning and implications of their own intellectual and spiritual character, and so they have collapsed the ground back into the hierarchy of structures of a dedivinized world.[28]

A complementary pattern, Voegelin would say, in general holds true for our relationship to the God of Jews and Christians. If one is incapable of undergoing for oneself, either through personal meditation or through sympathetic imagination, the pneumatic differentiations that impelled the tensional separation of the cosmos into transcendent God and mundane world, one will be unable to make proper sense of the reality imagined and conceived through Judeo-Christian categories and symbols. Nevertheless, the cosmos of the pagan gods is fled, and it cannot be recovered; our imaginal habitat is unmistakably the "disenchanted universe," in Max Weber's phrase. If the "living God of the fathers" is dead, then one is compelled to suffer the cramping of the ground of reality into the dimensions of that disenchanted universe, into desacralized space and time.

27. *The Ecumenic Age*, 236–37.
28. "In Search of the Ground," 13–16.

Voegelin writes of these phenomena often in terms of the "immanentization" of the transcendent ground. The ground is sought for in spatiotemporal reality once again:

> We still have, of course, the quest of the ground, we want to know where things come from. But . . . we can see, beginning about the middle of the eighteenth century, in the Enlightenment, a whole series of misplacements of the ground. The transcendent ground is misplaced somewhere in an immanent hierarchy of being. . . . [And we] can observe, for the last two hundred years, that every possible locale where one could misplace the ground has been exhausted.

Such a situation is inappropriately described as neopaganism, he observes, because the imputation of the ground to intracosmic forces and entities in traditional mythic thought is only superficially similar to the imputation of the ground to some portion of the dedivinized universe experienced as an "It" and not, without disingenuousness, as a "Thou." In the former case, human existence is consciously related, albeit compactly, to the divine mystery of its own ground: it is free to experience emotionally, and to portray for itself, its own givenness as mysteriously fulfilling a destiny ordained by the encompassing purposive powers of "the gods." In the latter case, however, human existence is alienated from any such purposive powers. The ground, whether identified with human reason or with some physical stratum of being, down to the subatomic particles or even a mysterious "energy," is not sacred. Sacred meaning and purpose have either dissolved in the impersonal determinisms of nature, or been absorbed into a human reason that must then cope with the problems of justifying a conception of itself as its own ground.[29]

Such cultural conditions Voegelin understands to offer enormous obstacles to recognizing the tension of existence as the in-between of finite and divine reality, and so to finding existential orientation through the classical symbols, philosophical or spiritual, that were designed to provide guidance into and within the "truth of existence." In the modern context, the tension of existence might be said, in his view, to be bent back upon itself or upon its disenchanted biological or material foundations, regularly discharging in outbursts of irrationalism and aggression

29. Ibid.; *The New Science of Politics,* 107.

its frustrated efforts to experience its own meaning as participating in a yet more meaningful story, a mysteriously complete and redemptive story, being told by the Whole, by divine reality. Voegelin's analysis leads to the conclusion that, in the context of a cultural horizon whose imaginal and conceptual contours have been shaped by philosophical and Judeo-Christian insights, the alternative to an existential ordering of consciousness through ascertainment and affirmation of a transcendent ground of being is the interpretation of existence as participating only in a story that is random, or mechanistically determined, or as ephemeral as human consciousness appears to be under its conditions of mortality—in short, a story that is absurd.

The Beyond and the Beginning

The ancient myths of origins, it was asserted, serve to situate fragile human existence in the enduring, comprehensive story being told by reality through "remembering" and retelling the divine events that took place in the Beginning, which ordained the necessary dispensation of things. But when experiences of transcendence have made symbolization of the ground in terms of sensual imagery emotionally and intellectually unconvincing, it becomes possible—indeed inevitable—for questions about primordial Beginnings to lead to the notion of a something "before" the existence of finite, imaginable things.

But here thinking runs into something of a paradox. What we mean by "time" is the condition of duration, or endurance, of the universe we inhabit. If experiences of transcendence bring to our attention a ground that is extra-spatiotemporal, then divine creation, which produced the world and its time, must have occurred "before" time. In other words, the differentiation of consciousness forces the speculative severance of all mundane events from the "act" or "acts" of sacred creation, and it compels the latter to be understood as a mysterious occurrence that "happened," as it were, before time. This paradoxical symbolization of a "Beginning before time" ought not to be dismissed as irrational, Voegelin insists, as it is a reasonable outgrowth of the differentiation of consciousness, but it does need to be informed by the critical realization that it expresses both a fact and a mystery. The fact is that a transcendent ground is responsible for the coming into being of this universe; the mystery is constituted by our knowing that we can have no direct conception or understanding of this "process," since human consciousness cannot directly conceive of a process that is not intrinsically temporal. What we can understand, then, is that our apprehension of the "event" of such a creation is analogical: that we are applying spatial and temporal categories to what we know can only indirectly and inadequately be represented by them. It is possible, therefore, to tell with honesty and conviction the "story" of a Creation that originates outside of time and outside of space, as the Judeo-Christian tradition of a creation ex nihilo does, while recognizing that it involves the use of imperfect analogy, that it is, in fact, a kind of mythos—but a mythos, be it well noted, that is informed by and is in harmony with critical-rational questioning and spiritually differentiated insights. Voegelin has spelled out, with admirable clarity, the sequence of insights just adumbrated:

> As he moves back on the time line, [man the questioner] will discover the regress to be indefinite. He will not find a divine beginning in time. The ground he is seeking is to be found, not in the things of the cosmos and their time dimension, but in the mystery of a creative beginning of the cosmos in a time out of time. Still, when the seeker makes the discovery, he will not abandon the directional index but use it analogically to symbolize the divinely-creative beginning of a reality that has a time dimension after all. The creational Beginning as an analogical symbol will denote therefore not a beginning in the time dimension of the world, but a beginning in the analogical time of a creation story.[30]

Mythoi of creation are not rendered obsolete, therefore, Voegelin's analysis shows, by the new truths revealed by critical reason and differentiated spirituality. On the contrary, some story of the genesis of the cosmos from the divine ground—what Voegelin calls in The Ecumenic Age a "cosmogonic myth"—remains in his view a permanent requirement of healthy, inquiring consciousness, expressing our trust and our understanding that we are participants in a story that embraces, transcends, and completes us. Such a mythos cannot reasonably be replaced either by a literal, "scientific" account of "creation" (since the nature of a transcendent Beginning transcends our comprehension), or by a simple refusal to

30. "The Beginning and the Beyond," 174.

offer any answer at all to the question as to why and wherefrom existence in the cosmos has come to pass (since we are granted enough knowledge about reality to fashion a story that satisfies our existential perspective). Rather, the mythoi can be, and have been, adjusted in accordance
with the differentiations of consciousness. The archaic cosmogonies "in
strictly cosmological form in which the divine presence is symbolized by
the intracosmic gods" have given way in the Western philosophical and
spiritual traditions to "cosmogonies in which these gods have been affected, to a lesser or greater degree, by the spiritual outbursts which
locate divine reality in the Beyond of all intramundane content."[31]

Voegelin argues that it is the Judeo-Christian tradition, and not Platonic-Aristotelian insights (or Eastern spiritual discoveries), that achieves
the most thorough differentiation with respect to divine-cosmic origins.
In *The Ecumenic Age,* he explains that in John's Gospel the Creator God
of Genesis 1, who created all reality through his Word, is identified with
the divine presence in the consciousness of Jesus, which is, Voegelin
would say, maximally differentiated for its radical transcendence. That
is, the Word of the Beginning that spoke reality into being is, in John's
telling, the very same "word from the Beyond" that speaks now through
the consciousness of Jesus, the word that calls each person to "eternal
life," to a meaning that is not "of the cosmos" but is, as Jesus gives as-
surance, "victorious over the cosmos." Through the epiphany of Christ,
as Voegelin sees it, the divine Beginning is taken to its utmost remove
from the cosmic stream of being and becoming.[32]

It is not the intention here to investigate Voegelin's thought in its relation to Christian theology. The salient point is that growing illumination
about the transcendent nature of the ground both does and does not alter
our relationship to cosmic Beginnings. It changes nothing in that some
notion of a Beginning is still required in order to make sense of reality;
but that notion itself changes as the spiritual and recondite character of
the creation of the cosmos is more and more fully realized.

Beyond these facts, however, there is a related, but more subtle and
more disturbing consequence that follows from these developments.
This is the fact that a certain tension, as Voegelin calls it, emerges be-

31. *The Ecumenic Age,* 11.
32. Ibid., 14, 17. Voegelin's interpretation centers on John 1 and 8.

tween (1) the divine ground insofar as it is experienced as the ordering presence that has made and still makes the cosmos what it is and (2) the divine ground as that furtherance of meaning, value, and reality discerned to be supraworldly in the questioning and yearning consciousness of human beings. The divine ground both forms the world *and* is a meaning that transcends it. And since humans are the foundations-inclusive site in finite reality where the illumination of the Whole transpires, it can be said that all finitude representatively becomes, *through the acts of differentiation that are occasioned by the search for the true ground,* aware of its own movement toward transcendent reality. It appears that finite reality is engaged, through the human search for meaning, in its transformation in the direction of the perfection of the Beyond. "Reality in this comprehensive sense is experienced as engaged in a movement of transcending itself in the direction of eminent reality."[33]

This is perhaps in Voegelin's view the central mystery of existence. Divine reality, the reality of the ground, is, he writes, "experienced in the two modes of the Beyond and the Beginning." The locus, the medium, of the discovery of the divine ground as the Beginning is the palpable cosmos, which presents itself as a fact demanding causal explanation: it is "the whole [which is] transparent for the presence of the divine ground." But the experience of the divine ground as a Beyond, as transcendent meaning, in the differentiating insights reveals "the manifold of existent things [to be] in tension toward the non-existent ground." In other words, the divinely created cosmos is dynamically oriented toward "a more eminent degree of reality" than exists in the created cosmos. Or, as Voegelin puts it, reality is structured in such a way that, through the differentiating insights, it is recognized to be moving beyond its present structure. Or again one might say: the meaning incarnate in the spatiotemporal universe and in finite consciousness is dynamically related to a supraworldly reality that is its completion, fulfillment, or perfection of meaning. Thus Voegelin concludes that the process of "transfiguration," or "eschatological movement," is at the heart of the story being told by reality.[34] The mystery of this state of affairs is put best by Voegelin in a brief passage in *The Ecumenic Age*:

33. Ibid., 216.
34. Ibid., 17, 78, 227, 258, 271.

There is a cosmos in which man participates by his existence; man is endowed with cognitive consciousness of the reality in which he is a partner; consciousness differentiates in a process called history; and in the process of history man discovers reality to be engaged in a movement toward the Beyond of its present structure. A cosmos that moves from its divine Beginning toward a divine Beyond of itself is mysterious indeed.[35]

Further discussion of Voegelin's conception of human existence as conscious participation in a mystery of transfiguration, and of the need for mythic symbolization of that mystery, will be necessary in order, in the following chapter, to show how this analysis of the experiences of transcendence informs a conception of "history" that is rather at odds with our commonsense understanding of the term. History is not, for Voegelin, the mere unfolding of events, human or otherwise, on a time line. It is the *pattern of the meaning of human existence* as it unfolds under temporal conditions; and that pattern of meaning, in his view, takes its decisive form from the differentiating experiences that reveal the eschatological tension in finite reality.

35. Ibid., 19.

· 3 ·

THE DRAMA OF HISTORY

History, it may be argued, is Voegelin's ultimate theoretical concern. Just as his theory of consciousness is the stable core of his larger, more comprehensive analysis of existence as the ongoing search for meaning, so that analysis forms part of an even broader design, which is the philosophy of history developed and presented in the five volumes of *Order and History*.

To describe Voegelin's overarching accomplishment as a "philosophy of history," however, is apt to give rise to misunderstanding, since the phrase suggests that he offers an interpretation of the overall meaning and goal of history. Also, ever since its invention in the eighteenth century, the title has typically referred to systematic accounts of universal history that are "scientific" in the sense of being secular in orientation, expressly intended to provide alternatives to the Christian interpretation of history that dominated Western speculation on history from Augustine to Bossuet. Voegelin's "philosophy of history" does not conform on either count. It does not provide a definitive answer concerning the meaning of history. And, as previous chapters have intimated, it is very specifically a philosophy concerned with the fact and the meaning of human response to, and conscious participation in, the divine ground of reality; thus it is hardly "secular," though Voegelin would certainly consider it "scientific" in the precise, classical sense of the word.[1] Unlike

1. For Voegelin's understanding and defense of the classical meaning of "science," see his introduction to *The New Science of Politics*.

70

other, typically modern "philosophies of history," then, Voegelin's emphasizes both the mystery of history as an unfinished process and the mystery of transcendent being that resides at its core.

From early in his career, the guiding principle of Voegelin's approach to history was his conviction that the "data" of history, the "material" to be made sense of, is not some blind process of events in the human or perhaps the cosmic field, but *the significant constants and variables in the self-interpretation of human existence over time.* Historical science, then, is a great deal more than the accurate recording of past events; it is, on the broadest scale, the effort to understand both the content and the development of "humanity's articulation of the meaning and purpose of existence."[2] In this view, the intelligibility of history is the overall pattern to be found in the unfolding process of human self-interpretation.

Given this approach, it is understandable that Voegelin from the beginning objected to the idea that history is properly conceived of as a unilinear process, a continuous march of humankind through primitive, ancient, medieval, and modern periods. If notable developments in human self-understanding are the key variables in history, one must acknowledge the problem of parallel "histories": as Western civilization was unfolding in the Near East, a Chinese civilization was simultaneously unfolding in the East, the two quite ignorant of each other; which, then, in terms of historical advance, was the carrier of meaning for its particular time phase in history? The answer has to be both—and so we must recognize that historical meaning does not simply unroll down a time line, but includes "cross-cut patterns" that unite spatially distant but contemporaneous societies. In other words, meaning in history involves, in addition to diachronic patterns unfolding on a time line, synchronic configurations that intelligibly structure history not back-to-forward, but "sideways," as it were. Therefore, to speak accurately of "meaning in history," one must keep both linear and cross-cut patterns together in view.[3]

But this is a relatively minor adjustment to have to make to our commonplace notion of history compared with what Voegelin's fully mature

2. Stephen A. McKnight, "The Evolution of Voegelin's Theory of Politics and History, 1944–1975," 33.
3. *The Ecumenic Age,* 2–5; McKnight, "The Evolution of Voegelin's Theory," 42–43.

conception demands of us. For when history is rigorously conceived in the above manner—not as a sequence of material events to be empirically verified and duly cataloged, but as a pattern of "lines of meaning" that emerge from the efforts of persons and societies to understand the structure of reality—then a significant factor in history is the relation of human beings, through participation, to a strictly transcendent source of being and truth. Because of this relation, an "eschatological line of meaning" appears in human self-understanding, and it takes its place in the process of self-discovery through the differentiation of consciousness. For the historian, whose concern is the development of human self-understanding, this renders the overall pattern of history extremely complex, since meaning in history must now be conceived as constituted not only by diachronically and synchronically related temporal structures, but also by the eschatological line of meaning that runs, so to speak, between the entire temporal field of unfolding meaning and the ground of reality beyond time. And as the eminent reality of the ground must dominate any interpretation of meaning in existence, the historian, in the interpretation of the human developments with which he or she is concerned, must accord special significance to those discoveries through which that eschatological line of meaning has come to be known and to the consequences of those discoveries.[4]

Voegelin's philosophy of history as laid out in his major works follows these principles of interpretation, although some of their deeper implications only gradually became fully realized and incorporated into the explicit analysis. In *The New Science of Politics* and the first three volumes of *Order and History,* the overall pattern of meaning in history is indeed presented as dominated by the discoveries of transcendent divine being, the "spiritual outbursts" that inaugurated a largely traumatic restructuring of human self-interpretation. In these works the explicit discoveries of a dimension of meaning beyond space and time—the "advance from compact to differentiated experiences of reality"—are presented as the central events for understanding the meaning of the unfolding of human existence in time. Two decades later, however, in the next volume of *Order and History, The Ecumenic Age,* Voegelin explains that even the original plan for organizing the materials in *Order and History* so as

4. *The Ecumenic Age,* 3.

to follow a chronological "course" of history from past to present is an indication of the extent to which he had still not broken free, up through the writing of the first three volumes, from an essentially linear, and therefore inadequate, conception of history. In its introduction, he states the hard facts: the form of an adequate philosophy of history "is definitely not a story of meaningful events to be arranged on a time line." The significant patterns of meaning in history as they have "revealed themselves in the self-interpretations of persons and societies" force the truly adequate analysis "to move backward and forward and sideways" as well as in what might be called the vertical direction of transcendent meaning. History is not, Voegelin states finally, a mere course of development, however complex, but a "web of meaning with a plurality of nodal points."[5] In other words, the traditional conception of history as *essentially* a movement of meaning from past to future is inadequate, because it obscures the synchronic and eschatological elements that also constitute historical meaning. Of course, there would be no history without the advances in self-interpretation that unfold as a process in time. But, Voegelin would argue, with the synchronic and especially the eschatological lines of meaning properly taken into consideration, it is no longer appropriate to describe the structure of history in general as a course; the course from past to future must be considered as one dimension of a "web of meaning" that only as a whole makes up "history."

History as Transfiguration

One of the foremost aims of *The Ecumenic Age* is to introduce and explain in some detail a conception of history properly consistent with the principles just discussed. It represents the theoretical fulfillment of a long development in Voegelin's preoccupation with historical meaning. In order to summarize its central conclusions, it would be well to begin with a few observations about the general concept of "human history."

Such a notion presupposes three principal facts. First, it presupposes a "subject" of history that includes all human beings who have ever lived or will live, at all times and in all places: it is the history not of this or of that

5. Ibid., 1–6, 57.

society, or cycle of societies, but of universal humankind. Second, it pre-supposes that something *changes* in that subject—that human existence in society does not just repeat itself mechanically, adorned with the acci-dental features of diverse cultures, but in fact admits of substantive de-velopmental transformations. The most important transformations will be the key variables in the process of history. Third, and finally, if there is to be a subject of history, and not a sequence of subjects, it must still remain the same humanity both before and after its developmental trans-formations; humanity must enjoy a constancy of nature that does *not* change through history, but provides a transhistorical basis for its histor-ical transformations. We can proceed by clarifying Voegelin's position on both the truth and the substance of each of these three presupposi-tions, beginning with the last, and moving in reverse sequence:

(1) For Voegelin, the abiding and comprehensive constant in human existence is the search for meaning. "What is permanent in the history of mankind is . . . man himself in search of his humanity and its order."[6] This permanent search for truth and order to which Voegelin refers is the immediate and ongoing dynamic principle of each individual and every society, insofar as existence is a struggle for the experience of mean-ingfulness, of meaning fulfilled. This is a struggle that, of course, en-counters numerous obstacles along the way. Ignorance, a corrupt social environment, the misuse of freedom, all of these may contribute to an experience of living, not in a plenitude of reality known and loved, but in a vacuum of falsehood and disorder. As Voegelin would say, it is possible for the tension of conscious participation to fall out of "attunement" with the order of being in which it exists. Therefore, the search for meaning, while a constant, is always

> a disturbing movement in the In-Between of ignorance and knowledge, of time and timelessness, of imperfection and perfection, of hope and fulfillment, and ultimately of life and death. From the experience of this movement, from the anxiety of losing the right direction in this In-Between of darkness and light, arises the inquiry concerning the mean-ing of life. But it does arise only because life is experienced as man's participation in a movement with a direction to be found or missed.[7]

6. "Equivalences of Experience," 115.
7. "The Gospel and Culture," 176.

(2) If this is the invariable structure of existence, it follows that the variables that order this constancy into "history" must involve changes in this search for meaning—in the way it is experienced, understood, symbolized, and fulfilled or thwarted—that alter it in such a way that, while it is the same search, one must say that it has undergone a profound developmental transformation. For Voegelin, the preeminent change in this regard, before which others retreat into relative insignificance, is constituted by the transformation from compact mythic thinking into differentiated consciousness: in the West, into rationally differentiated consciousness, beginning with the Greeks, and into spiritually differentiated consciousness, beginning in Israel. When, under the pressure of questioning, the transcendence of the ground, along with the rational and spiritual centers of personality through which it is able to be discerned, originally came into view, the traditional mythic symbols through which the order of reality was understood by compact consciousness began to lose power as guiding and convincing answers to the search for meaning. The shock of these developments, stretched out over centuries (and in fact continuing into the present), can scarcely be overestimated. For they called for a new mode of participation in reality, in which one is oriented by new insights and symbols corresponding to the discovery and exploration of the interior rational or spiritual personality—the "mind" or "spirit"—and to the revelations of a ground of reality that lies beyond the visible, the imaginable, the figurable, the spatial and temporal. The inadequacy of the traditional mythic answers and symbols for mediating the sense of existence and for guiding action in the face of these discoveries induced an acute and protracted disequilibrium (again continuing into the present) as the condition out of which a new equilibrium had to be sought.[8]

Now, it is in part these developments, according to Voegelin, that first engendered an awareness of history in the sense of a radical, irreversible, and unique change of "epoch" or "era." This is because the differentiating insights were experienced as irreversibly changing *and advancing* the human search for attunement with the Whole and its divine ground. The emergence of historical consciousness in a profound sense involved the emphatic awareness of advancing from a less true into a more true mode

8. Corrington, "Order and Consciousness," 160.

of conscious participation in reality. As Voegelin has expressed it, "Human existence in society has history because . . . social order is an attunement of man with the order of being, and because this order can be understood by man and realized in society with increasing approximations to its truth." Indeed, the discoveries of transcendence in Israel and Hellas were experienced as such decisive transformations in human self-understanding that they evoked descriptions of themselves as transitions from "death" (existence informed by the traditional understanding and the social conditions reflecting it) to "life" (personal and social existence transformed by the new insights):

> Moses led Israel from the death of bondage to the life of freedom under God. Plato discovered life for the erotic souls and punishment for the dead souls. Christianity discovered the faith that saves man from the death of sin and lets him enter, as a new man, into the life of the spirit. In every instance of a present in historical form, the Either-Or of life and death divides the stream of time into the Before-and-After of the great discovery.[9]

So it is "historical" awareness that recognizes the need for and undertakes the tortuous resymbolization of reality in light of the differentiating insights, and which is thereby forced to cope with the question as to how to relate the prior and the new dispensations in such a way that the "advance" itself can be understood as meaningful and proper.

(3) Finally, there is the question about what, or who, it is that suffers these advances: who is the subject of historical transformations? Formulating the question implies that all humans at all times can reasonably be considered to be a single community, sharing an essence that binds together uncountably diverse personal and social existences, and that the meaning of each is bound to the meaning of all. But what is the empirical basis for this extraordinary assumption, that our lives take their meaning

9. *The World of the Polis*, 2; *Israel and Revelation*, 130–31. One should note Voegelin's repeated insistence that, while apprehension of the transcendent nature of the ground was a necessary condition for producing a consciousness of history intense enough to produce historiography, it was only the "triad" of (1) the discovery of transcendence, (2) the emergence of historiography, and (3) the rise of an ecumenic empire threatening the absorption of smaller societies in its path, that together made up a "unit of experience" capable of inspiring consciousness of epochal advance. See *The Ecumenic Age*, 308–16.

in part from their participation in "universal humankind," that all human destinies are united by more than their biological and generic identity and have a place in a common human story?

Voegelin's answer begins with the obvious but important observation that universal humankind is not a "concrete society." What is it then? It is a notion, an image, a symbol that gradually appears in Western culture, arising from the realization that there is, in fact, a common human element that transcends environmental, biological, psychological, and societal circumstances—an element, in other words, not intrinsically conditioned by the accidents of space and time. The recognition of such a common element depends, naturally, on speculative transcendence of the imaginal horizon of spatiotemporal existence—and with this one has penetrated to the heart of the matter. Only the differentiating insights that expose the participation of human beings in a transcendent ground can render a conception of humanity as one community, sharing one essence. The community of reason (*nous*), as conceived in the Greek philosophical tradition, or the community of spirit (*pneuma*), as understood by the early Christian communities, reaches beyond the material foundations of individual members, because *nous* and *pneuma* are conceived, respectively, as the very substance of transcendent divinity. Universal humanity comes into view simultaneously with universal divinity: human beings are essentially related to each other because each shares in a "flux of divine presence," as Voegelin calls it, that relates them to a single pole of the one transcendent being. And so a "scattering of societies belonging to the same biological type . . . is discovered to be one mankind with one history, by virtue of participation in the same flux of divine presence." Therefore, "universal mankind is not a society existing in the world, but a symbol which indicates man's consciousness of participating, in his earthly existence, in the mystery of a reality that moves toward its transfiguration."[10]

Voegelin's theory, then, explains that consciousness of history in the precise sense of epochal advances in the human search for truth and order arises from a constellation of cognitive events, which includes: (1) the discoveries about human nature and reality connected with the revelation of the transcendence of the divine ground; (2) the recognition on

10. *The Ecumenic Age*, 6, 305.

the part of their recipients that these discoveries constitute an epochal advance in insight; and (3) the revelation of universal humankind that in these very discoveries is recognized to be searching, in advancing stages of clarity, for its meaning in relation to the one divine ground.

And what then, for Voegelin, is history in the most general and complete sense, given this analysis? His response may be indicated by drawing out the implications of a theoretical equation he makes during one of his discussions of St. Augustine's theology of history: "The structure of history is the same as the structure of personal existence."[11]

A person's existence gathers its meaning as it unfolds in time. Until its life in time is finished, the meaning of its existence is incomplete. But every person's existence is a striving for fulfillment not merely in its worldly but also in its transcendent meaning. The complete pattern of meaning concerning an individual's existence is therefore constituted, one must say, by the meaning of events that unfold in time (including all synchronic relationships) and then also by the relation of this complete configuration to the meaning of the transcendent ground, from which it derives its being and in which it seeks (knowingly or not) its perfection.

Similarly, history is the complete process, as yet unfinished, of human meaning unfolding in time, in which diachronic and synchronic lines of meaning point to their fulfillment, penultimately in the completion of that process, but ultimately in the relation of the whole configuration of meaning to the transcendent, mysterious meaning of the Whole. Personal existence, as conscious participation in the divine ground, is structured as an orientation toward a fulfillment of meaning beyond time and space; history, as the common field of human participation in the ground, is likewise structured. And as personal existence can undergo a "leap" of conversion when it recognizes and accepts its own orientation toward transcendence—a leap that marks the central event in the story of its career in temporal existence—so in history a people or persons can undergo, representatively for all humanity, similar leaps, which mark, in the time of history, the decisive events in the human search for meaning. For Voegelin, the "spiritual outbursts" of Israel and Hellas, as well as those of the India of the Upanishads and the Buddha, and the China of Confucius and the Taoist sages, are such decisive events in terms of the

11. "Immortality," 78.

process of history, as initial revelatory breakthroughs; *but meaning in history is ultimately affected by every act of human participation in the divine ground.* History is the entire pattern of human-divine encounter stretched out through time. It is "a pattern of timeless moments," in the words of T. S. Eliot.[12]

The conclusions to which the foregoing analysis leads converge on one central theme, reiterated throughout *The Ecumenic Age:* the historical pattern of meaning originates in the variety of human responses to the presence of the divine ground, and the decisive variation in those responses involves the ground compelling its own properly transcendent—and properly rational, free, loving, and creative—nature to become known and responded to in finite consciousness. History is, therefore, in Voegelin's view, the unfolding story of divine revelation through time: "'History' in the sense of an area in reality in which the insight into the meaning of existence advances is the history of theophany." "The history of man . . . is transacted in a permanent present as the ongoing drama of theophany."[13]

What, then, is the meaning *of* history? What can we know of it as a complete process?

Of the "meaning of history" as a whole, Voegelin tells us, we can say nothing definite at all, for two reasons: human existence in time is still unfolding, and so the full pattern of its meaning is still "open toward the future"; and again, that meaning is shrouded in the mystery of its transcendent origins and goal. But this does not mean we know nothing of its direction and sense. What can be discerned of that purpose may be summarized in the most general fashion by saying that it involves a transformation from pre-differentiated consciousness to consciousness emphatically aware of its existence in relation to a meaning that transcends the meaning incarnate in the finite cosmos. And this means that, in Voegelin's view, reality as a whole is engaged in a process of "transfiguration." This is a transfiguration taking place specifically through acts of consciousness, in which specific areas of finite reality—specific conscious existences—are drawn into a conscious participation in a full-

12. "Little Gidding" (*Four Quartets,* 58). Voegelin quotes the phrase approvingly in "Immortality," 77.
13. *The Ecumenic Age,* 226, 252.

ness of being beyond space and time. We can't be certain of the goal of the process—its unfinished and transcendent meaning eludes us—but we can know that it involves the truth about the relation between finite reality and its transcendent ground emerging into affirming consciousness. The transfiguration Voegelin has in mind appears to be a precarious participation, in the medium of consciousness, of generated and perishing being in the imperishable being of the transcendent ground.

Why "precarious"? Because, while our own experiences of temporally conditioned participation in the pole of transcendent being may lead us to imagine the process of history culminating in a completed and stable transfiguration of some kind, perhaps consisting of personal existences—or the world itself—achieving a state of nonperishing fulfillment, we have no evidence of such a stasis or fulfillment. History is an "in-between" kind of reality: it evidences a process of transition, or transformation, and while it has clearly embarked on a journey, it just as clearly has not reached the destination toward which it appears to be heading. Critical awareness of the historical dimension in reality "reveals existence as neither transfigured nor untransfigured but as engaged in a transfiguring movement." In other words, so far as one can tell, the transfiguring process is itself static, in the sense that "it [has lasted] through the millennia of known history to this day"; thus one can affirm that the intelligibility of historically dynamic reality includes the stable structure of perishable, finite, imperfect meaning *becoming* translated into a more eminent mode of participation in the imperishable divine ground of meaning. This is the intelligible configuration that Voegelin calls "the paradox of a recognizably structured process that is recognizably moving beyond its structure."[14]

Finally, it should be stressed that, for Voegelin, all of the strata of finite reality are implicated in the meaning that accrues to historical transformation. As he explains, the distinguishable levels of finite being, from the inorganic particles studied by modern physics up through the organic and conscious realms, are not "a number of strata one piled on top of the other," but a consubstantial field organized as a hierarchy of structures in which higher, more inclusive or more comprehensive, forms embrace and augment the meanings of the lower forms that provide their

14. "Wisdom," 336; *The Ecumenic Age,* 227.

foundations. Therefore, "by virtue of their founding character, the lower strata reach into the stratum of human consciousness, not as its cause but as its condition," which in turn makes "the process of history to extend structurally, through participation, into the other strata of reality, including the physical universe."[15] The whole of finite reality is implicated ontologically in the "eschatological movement" that is known and enacted in the tension of consciousness as it shares in, to the extent that is humanly possible, the divine ground beyond all generated and perishing things.

History and Mythos

Order and History begins with a singularly poignant metaphor: every human being, Voegelin writes, is an actor in "the drama of being," who must play his or her role in ignorance of its essential meaning. The full meaning of the role cannot be known because its essence is the function it serves in the meaning of the drama as a whole, while the drama as a whole cannot be known because the only perspective available to the actor is from within the unfolding story. The story has neither begun with, nor will end with, the actor's existence. Rather, one is lifted temporarily into the obligation to act appropriately, with the freedom at one's disposal, in the ongoing action, whose origin and outcome remain a mystery.

As Voegelin immediately goes on to emphasize, this "ultimate essential ignorance is not complete ignorance." The dramatic metaphor is applicable, in fact, because to be human means to recognize, and to partially comprehend, one's situation within being, and to have the freedom to orient oneself in light of available knowledge about its order and significance. So we can say that human beings are able, because of limited but real knowledge, to attempt to shape the roles they have been granted in a way that seems fitting in light of what the drama of being is understood to require.[16]

Voegelin has described this task or adventure of the actor as a seeking of "attunement" with what is most real and most permanent in reality.

15. *The Ecumenic Age,* 334–35.
16. *Israel and Revelation,* 1–2.

The cosmos, with its sets of objects, relationships, rhythms, and laws, is given; our lives and consciousnesses are given amid the fabric of the cosmic processes, from which they emerge and with which they seek to assimilate that which is constituted by human knowledge and human action; and suffering and action are experienced as meaningful when they are felt or known to be not in discord with the font of power—the "will of the gods," or the *ma'at,* or the Tao, or the Logos—that unchangingly orders all things to their ends. "Attunement [is] the state of existence when it hearkens to that which is lasting in being, when it maintains a tension of awareness for its partial revelations in the order of society and the world, when it listens attentively to the silent voices of conscience and grace in human existence itself." In traditional mythic societies, attunement revolved around the ritual coordination of social and personal existence with the intentions of gods or cosmic powers, by means of the mediating explanations and solace of ritual-directing myths. The sanction on such performative attunement was for the member of archaic societies what Voegelin has called "the horror of a fall from being": the experience, marked by anxiety and despair, of one's participation becoming, through a "mismanagement of existence," a disorder or vacant routine cut off from the divine sources of truth and reality—a non-participation. To lose attunement is to become alienated from the meaning of the encompassing drama.[17]

In this regard, time and history have changed nothing. For Voegelin, the pole and counterpole of attunement and alienation remain constants in human experience under all historical circumstances, as do the moods that belong to each of them and the vicissitudes of the struggle in which the one must be achieved and the other avoided or overcome. But the differentiated awareness of transcendent being has radically altered the requirements of attunement. Now the human actor who wishes to overcome the anxiety endemic to having a role to play in the drama of being must cope with adjusting his or her performance to an "unseen measure"—to a standard for action that, because rooted in transcendent being, is discernable only in conscience, refinement of feeling, and the invisible, delicate procedures of personal judgment with their well-known

---

17. Ibid., 4–5, 9–10.

risks of ignorance, self-deception, and rationalization.[18] The price paid
for the historical advance of insight into the order of reality that was
achieved by the rational and spiritual differentiations of consciousness is
the greatly intensified precariousness of the link between the truth of the
ground and the human effort to fashion existence into true participation.

And those advances have shown that the drama of being is a history:
that its story line includes the progression, in the course of time, to superior apprehensions of truth. The knowing participant in history thus is
obliged, in the struggle for attunement, to advance with the advancing
insights. And since a differentiated awareness of transcendent reality is
the essence of the advance, this means that the individual must open
himself or herself to the bewilderment, disorientation, and reorientation
that are entailed in the passage from a compact interpretation of reality
to a life informed by the truths conveyed by the philosophical and spiritual insights into transcendent reality. Why one happens to be born
later, and not earlier, in time, and so bears responsibility for raising one's
existence up to the level of these insights is, of course, a mystery—and in
the contemporary world, where (as Voegelin sees it) the traditions meant
to guide and impart these insights have become almost unrecognizable
under the incrustation of the new and compelling compact vision of reality as the "physical universe" studied by the collective natural sciences,
it seems particularly hard that attunement demands such a personal
achievement. But one has no choice in the matter: "[O]nce the discovery
[of transcendence] is made, it is endowed with the quality of an authori-
tative appeal to every man to actualize it in his own soul." However
unpropitious social and cultural conditions may appear to be, one is
not permitted, within the authority of historical developments, to go
back of the advances and "play existence in cosmic-divine order"—that
is, pretend that the discoveries of transcendent meaning have never taken
place, and that the physical cosmos is felt to be ultimate reality—even
when "cosmic-divine order" is merely being imitated, as in modernity,

18. The symbolism of the "unseen measure," of which Voegelin is particularly
fond, derives from the Greek statesman, legislator, and poet Solon. His understanding
of human virtue (*arete*) as action in accordance with the just will of the gods, a will
known only through "the unseen measure of right judgment," is discussed by Voegelin
in *The World of the Polis*, 194–99.

by the "compactness" of various materialisms, psychologisms, or vague pantheisms.[19]

This does not mean, however, that attunement to the drama of history consists of a philosophical penetration of the intelligible structure of the advances. What is required is a life *informed* by the differentiating insights; and that formation typically and appropriately takes place through the effective mediation of the meaning of those insights by imaginal representations of the truths they reveal about reality. Existential attunement is always primarily a matter of spontaneous imaginative engagement in the drama of being, in which we connect the story lines of our lives, not through calm and reflective analysis, but immediately and massively through the feelings associated with certain images and symbols, with the encompassing drama of the Whole. Today the drama of the Whole is known to include history; history is part of the larger story, the mysterious story, being told by reality. Only, therefore, by seeking and finding a convincing set of images and symbols, a mythos, of the Whole, a "likely story" of the ultimate meaning of both being and history, with which one's imagination and feelings can fully resonate, can the contemporary individual find the solace and joy of attunement.

Throughout *The Ecumenic Age,* Voegelin discusses the refinement of mythoi dealing with cosmic and human destiny as they came to be transformed, in various traditions, from their archaic variants to compatibility with the truths of philosophy, spirit, and history. In the course of that discussion he introduces the theme of the changing "horizon" of conscious existence.

Horizon, as Voegelin defines it here, is the border of "man's habitat in the cosmos" as it appears from the perspective of his awareness and understanding; it is the boundary of known reality. In archaic thought, the circumference of reality is closed by spatiotemporal imagination. The primal Beginning merges with the beginnings of everyday experience; the divine presence is not differentiated from the palpable cosmos; if there is an End to things, it too is a cataclysm (and perhaps renewal) in the same homogeneous medium as that in which plant and animal life reproduces and grows, the seasons change, and the planets move in their courses. But with the rational and spiritual differentiations of conscious-

---

19. *The World of the Polis,* 187; *Israel and Revelation,* 465.

ness, the horizon begins to recede, and does not stop receding until it becomes the border between the entire spatial and temporal field and the divine mystery beyond space and time. The mystery of transcendence becomes the circumference of reality: "The Horizon recedes so far that space and time become the *eikon* [image] of the spaceless and timeless ground of being."[20]

In other words, with the dissolution of the ancient mythic horizon, through differentiating insights and political events, a "new horizon of mystery" comes into view, one that breaks beyond the farthest reaches of the spatial cosmos and its temporal duration into another order of reality altogether, which is the mystery of transcendent meaning. Now when this occurs, the character of the "story" being told by reality, as understood by its human participants, is perforce required to undergo reinterpretation. More adequate, in the sense of more differentiated, mythoi are required that reflect the new awareness of the strictly transcendent horizon. An example of such a refinement of mythoi is the change in the portrayal of divine creation as we move from typical archaic Near Eastern myths to the Israelite account in Genesis. The latter has advanced from "the compact imagery of elemental, physiological, sexual, or materially demiurgic creativity to the symbolism of the creative word," a genuinely spiritual conception of both divinity and creation.[21] But in a cultural context (such as ours) well informed by the fruits of both the rational and spiritual differentiations, a truly convincing, comprehensive mythos must account not only for the spiritual nature of the divine ground and of divine creation but also for the mysterious, yawning gap between that world-transcendent divinity and the mundane world; it must account for the strange creature in whose consciousness that gap is both revealed and bridged; and no less, it must account for the historical advances of insight and the activity of transfiguration that history appears to entail.

20. *The Ecumenic Age*, 202–3, 208, 210–11. The metaphor of cosmic time as "the moving eikon of eternity" is found in Plato's *Timaeus* 37c–38b. Voegelin emphasizes that in this breakdown and widening of conscious horizon during the "ecumenic age," a crucial role is played by the impact of political enterprises of conquest and expansion, along with geographical exploration. The differentiation of consciousness and imperial expansion, in fact, are partners in causing the horizon of conscious existence to move beyond cosmological symbolism to the articulated border of transcendent mystery.

21. "The Beginning and the Beyond," 186.

In fact, Voegelin argues that when the process of history is properly understood as the transfiguration of finite reality through human-divine encounter, it is history itself—the unfolding process of divine reality revealing itself in human consciousness—that becomes the true "horizon of divine mystery."[22] And, if one may extrapolate from his arguments, he suggests that a mythos adequate to this recognition of historical process as the ultimate horizon of conscious existence will be a tale that addresses, from the perspective of the Whole, (1) the emergence of finite reality from a divine Beyond of transcendent meaning; (2) the emergence within finite reality of a creaturely locus in which the freedom and creativity of that reality which transcends spatial and temporal determination can become present, in order to work a transfiguration of finite reality in the direction of the more eminent reality of the divine Beyond; (3) the emergence of the effective realization of this presence within the carriers of transfiguration; and (4) the culmination of the historical process in a completed transfiguration. One must "extrapolate from his arguments," because nowhere does Voegelin describe, as I have just done, these four components as the structure of a mythos that would be fully complementary to his own philosophy of history. But in his discussion in *The Ecumenic Age* of what he calls the "Pauline myth"—the "tale of death and resurrection" that St. Paul preaches in the New Testament documents—each of these four components is identified and either explicitly or implicitly claimed by Voegelin to belong centrally to this "tale" that he considers "superior" to any other differentiated myths, including those of Plato.[23] If the logos of Voegelin's philosophy of history raises the question as to its correlative mythos, the following passages appear to me to be the closest thing to a direct answer to that question from Voegelin himself:

> If the movement of reality is consistently extrapolated toward its goal . . . [the correlative] myth must become the story of the fall from and return to the imperishable state of creation intended by divine creativity. . . . The Pauline myth indeed pursues the drama of the movement to its conclusion in the eschatological events. . . . The movement in reality, that has become luminous to itself in noetic conscious-

22. *The Ecumenic Age,* 313–16, 328–35.
23. Ibid., 239–60, 269; see especially 248–51.

ness, has indeed unfolded its full meaning in the Pauline vision and its exegesis through the myth. The symbolism of the man who can achieve freedom from cosmic Ananke [necessity], who can enter into the freedom of God, redeemed by the loving grace of the God who is himself free of the cosmos, consistently differentiates the truth of existence that has become visible in the philosophers' experience of *athanatizein* [immortalizing, i.e., participating in divine transcendence].[24]

Of course, such a mythos is no more than a story; and Voegelin criticizes St. Paul for an uncritical "blending" of the fabric of his tale, which tells how he and all who respond to Jesus' message will share in the imperishable glory of resurrection, with the fabric of life in the unresolved in-between of temporally conditioned human experience and the unfinished process of human history. That blending is very dangerous. It can lead to a literalization of the symbols of the "likely story" in a way that confuses them with the definite facts of existence, which in turn can inspire the confidence that nothing remains to be known about human existence or history—that their basic mysteries have been, not revealed, but answered. Such, Voegelin tirelessly repeats, is not the case. Why there is a drama of history, and what its outcome will be, are, equally, unknown and unknowable from the human perspective. The Pauline Christian mythos, like other mythoi in conformity with either the rational or the spiritual differentiations or with both, expresses a knowledge of divine transcendence, of human consciousness as divine-human encounter, and of that transfiguration in the world being suffered through divine initiative and human response that Voegelin calls history. But why history exists, why anyone must play a role in it, and what depends on his or her playing it well or ill—no one can answer with certainty.

Stated so flatly, the impressiveness of the mystery of history is hard to

---

24. Ibid., 250–51. McKnight, in "The Evolution of Voegelin's Theory," argues that Voegelin is "providing a whole new philosopher's myth" in the symbols of his work and claims that he "clearly is not an objective social analyst surveying other constructions [but rather] involved in the development of a mythos, a likely truth to counteract the distortions of the ideologies" (44). This assessment seems overhasty. Voegelin, I would argue, is providing in the reflective symbols of his work not *mythopoeic symbols* that tell a tale of reality, but *heuristic symbols* that invite readers to respond to already existing, exemplary mythoi regarding the process of reality, and that invite them as well to understand the complementary relationship between such mythoi and philosophical logoi.

deny. It is so impressive that it typically inspires the flight to certainty in its wide variety of modes, from the insistence that one particular mythos is in fact logos, to a commonplace resistance to the very fact of transcendent reality, to the modern fabrications of philosophies of history that claim comprehensive knowledge of the meaning of the Whole.

· 4 ·

MYSTERY AND MYTHOS

It is possible, now, to proceed to a systematic summary of Voegelin's analysis of the central mysteries of every human existence and of what is involved in recognizing and embracing them. This will entail further clarification, also, of Voegelin's understanding of the function and significance of the mythic symbolization of our existential situation. Because of the truth of mystery, the imaginatively compelling "likely story," or mythos, is regarded by Voegelin as an irreplaccable medium through which our apprehension of the meaning of human participation in the Whole may be satisfyingly expressed and made effective for personal and social orientation.

Transcendent Meaning and the Mysteries of Existence

There is no explicit recognition of a mystery, in the strict sense, without understanding that there are ultimacies of meaning that transcend human intelligence and imagination. Such a recognition means understanding, through a differentiating insight, that the universe of finite things and relations cannot reasonably be considered to be the origin and ground of its own existence and meaning. Only when the ground of reality is recognized or sensed to be non-finite and unconditioned, and therefore to be a real dimension of being of which we realize we can have no direct or substantive knowledge, is it possible to appreciate, explicitly, that what engenders and comprehends our lives is humanly unknowable, is mysterious in principle. The following summary of Voegelin's treatment of the mysteries of existence takes its bearings, accordingly, from the fact of transcendent meaning.

When the ground of being is explicitly understood to be unknowable, one discovers "a blind spot at the center of all human knowledge about man." Everything that pertains to "the decisive core" of one's life is haunted by the same dead center of ignorance, because the essence of existence has been revealed to be participation in a process whose ultimate meaning transcends human comprehension.[1] Our deepest concerns, therefore, lead us to mysteries, and four that are specified in Voegelin's writings are the mystery of origins, the mystery of personal meaning, the mystery of history, and the mystery of the relationship between individual destiny and universal history.

The mystery of origins is, from the differentiated perspective, the mystery of the How and Why of the emergence of a finite, conditioned universe from a non-finite, unconditioned ground. As Voegelin convincingly argues, there is no escaping the question of the ground itself, the question of what it is we ultimately "come from"; and differentiated reason demands that the presence of finite reality be accorded a non-finite origin or cause. The ultimate purpose of the coming-into-being, therefore, and the manner of its creation, are unknowable to us, transcending finite powers of comprehension. Even the general notions of "origination," "coming from," "creation," "causation," and "formation" can be applied to the relation between finite being and its transcendent ground only analogically; for the meanings of these terms derive from our understanding of relations between finite beings.

These, of course, are not novel truths. But Voegelin's treatment of the mystery of origins contains a further set of insights that marks a major contribution to the theoretical appreciation of the issue. These are the insights formulated in his analysis of the "Beginning" and the "Beyond."

Conscious existence, Voegelin explains, discovers through differentiating experiences that it receives its "formation" not merely through physical processes but also through the nonmaterial presences of *nous*

---

1. *Israel and Revelation*, 2.

and *pneuma*. For the seeker of origins, this discovery refracts the originating ground, as far as human existence is concerned, in the two "directions" of (1) the transcendent Beginning of cosmic structure (from which human consciousness arises) and (2) the transcendent Beyond of Intelligence or Spirit (which differentiated consciousness recognizes, in the immediacy of presence, as the fullness of its own rational and spiritual identity). Voegelin has carefully summarized this issue of the two directions in the following passage:

> Though the divine reality [of the ground] is one, its presence is experienced in the two modes of the Beyond and the Beginning. The Beyond is present in the immediate experience of movements in the psyche; while the presence of the divine Beginning is mediated through the experience of the existence and intelligible structure of things in the cosmos. The two models require two different types of language for their adequate expression. The immediate presence in the movements of the soul requires the revelatory language of consciousness [such as descriptions of questioning, searching, ignorance, knowledge, illumination, conversion and so on, while the] presence mediated by the existence and order of things in the cosmos requires the mythical language of a creator-god or Demiurge, of a divine force that creates, sustains, and preserves the order of things.[2]

Both "models" of the ground of reality are "required" by differentiated consciousness; but that simultaneous requirement can prove troublesome. The two, the cosmic ground of things and the "immediate" ground of consciousness, can appear to be in conflict. That is, once the invisible center of personality is differentiated, it is possible to speculate as to whether one's being as physical, as physically rooted in the cosmos, is not in conflict with one's being as beyond the physical, as moral or spiritual. To borrow Kant's words, the ground of "the starry heavens above me" sometimes seems to have a questionable relationship to the ground of "the moral law within me."[3] This problem of discordance engenders its own mysteries, to be discussed shortly.

2. *The Ecumenic Age*, 17–18.
3. Immanuel Kant, *Critique of Practical Reason*, 166. Voegelin refers to these formulations in *The Ecumenic Age*, 77–78.

Secondly, there is the mystery involving the meaning of one's personal existence. Voegelin's philosophical anthropology explains that conscious existence is properly represented as the "tension" of a knowing questioning, of an informed search for meaning. But what meaning does the personal search for meaning ultimately have?

The definitive answer to such a question is, of course, wrapped in the mystery of the transcendent meaning that is both the origin of every person and the ultimate goal of his or her search. The fact, however, that individual consciousness is ontologically constituted as a "permanent presence of the tension toward eternal being, related to worldly time" raises a question about personal destiny. Voegelin, along with Plato and Aristotle, allows that philosophical understanding of the nature of consciousness raises a legitimate question about an "immortal" completion or fulfillment of the personal search for meaning. Plato, of course, examines the question of the possibly immortal status of the soul in numerous dialogues, and Aristotle, in a famous passage, urges his students to "become immortal [*athanatizein*] as far as that is possible" through nurturing the life of intellect (*nous*). Voegelin would contend that an adequate analysis of consciousness leads the question about personal meaning inexorably to the promise suggested in the fact that conscious existence is a human-divine participation.[4]

But Voegelin also points out that the philosophical understanding of consciousness as a tension of participation is poorly served, in a theoretical context, by simply attaching immortal status to the soul; and further, that it was Plato's and Aristotle's recognition of this very fact that led to their creation of "a host of new symbols [to] express the experience of an area of reality intermediate between God and man."[5] Nevertheless, since even in Voegelin's writings consideration of the goal of the personal search for meaning leads often enough to his approving use of the emotionally charged language of "immortality," it will be help-

---

4. *Anamnesis*, 133; Aristotle, *Nicomachean Ethics* 1177b32–33. Voegelin translates Aristotle's term *athanatizein* by the intransitive "to immortalize" because, in his view, "the symbol is meant to characterize noetic life as an habit of action by which man can, and ought to, increase his potential immortality to its full stature." According to Voegelin, this "practice of 'immortalizing' is to Aristotle a virtue superior to all other" ("Immortality," 88).

5. "Immortality," 89.

ful to pursue his analysis of the mystery of personal meaning from this particular angle.

Voegelin has written extensively on the idea and symbol of immortality, especially in "Immortality: Experience and Symbol" and a number of later articles, and his analysis may be reduced to two fundamental theses. First, human beings have been able to imagine "immortal life"—originally as an exclusive privilege of the gods, but eventually as a possible destiny for human souls in an afterlife or through a series of rebirths—because consciousness in fact experiences something in its own being that transcends what comes and goes in time. But second, the *imagery* of immortality, or afterlife, derives from "compact" or pre-differentiated imagination, which portrays reality, including nonperishing reality, in terms of entities occupying space and time. In a proper theoretical analysis, Voegelin argues, it is inappropriate to ask whether consciousness is mortal or immortal, because the terms denote qualities or characteristics of entities, and consciousness is not an entity. One must move beyond the hypostatic conception of consciousness if one desires a philosophical account of the matter.

When Voegelin employs the "in-between" symbolisms of Plato and Aristotle—the symbols of *participation* and of *metaxic existence*—to explain the structure of consciousness, he attempts to strip them completely of any connotations that associate them with the description of entities. When he states that consciousness may be said to be in-between finite and transcendent being, this in-between is not intended to be a spatial description; it symbolizes the reality of a dynamic matrix where finite and transcendent meaning meet and interpenetrate. As such, consciousness is neither a "thing" that passes, nor eminently divine; it is not identical with its material foundations, nor independent of those foundations. It is, he declares, the mystery of a "life" that, while subject to the death that belongs to it as a physical organism, also shares, through the ordering forces of reason and spirit, in the imperishable presence of the ground. Voegelin concentrates this into a single formula by stating that, unlike the passing of merely organic entities, human life "is *structured* by death." He goes on to explain: "The life structured by death is neither the life of the mortals, nor the lasting of the gods, but the life experienced in the tension of existence. It is the life lived in the flow of presence." "Presence" here is the timeless presence of the ground. It is a "flow" for humans, who encounter it as their deepest identity, but only as refracted in the medium of spatiotemporal existence. To be human is to be an intermediary between the world that passes and the ground that does not. Personal existence, under the only conditions in which we experience it, is an unresolved tension between "life and death, immortality and mortality, perfection and imperfection, time and timelessness."[6]

It follows, therefore, that an individual's life takes its consummate meaning from the role it plays in mediating the presence of the ground within finite existence. It is a role that, barring accident or abnormal circumstances, the individual has the capacity to shape. A person, for example, may turn away from the promises and obligations of his or her mediating status by stifling awareness of the ground, letting the search for meaning run aside into pleasures and divertissements for the sake of trying to escape from the anxieties and responsibilities of conscious existence. In Voegelin's view, certain choices and decisions are required if a human being is to play a genuinely human role in life; life lived may not be truly human "life" at all, but a routine based on the avoidance of one's consciousness of participating in that which transcends death. Nevertheless, the structure of consciousness is always that of an in-between, of a tension between immanence and transcendence, and however much one might wish to belong merely to one or the other of the two, to "this world" or to the "other world," to "flesh" or to "spirit," the fact remains that these opposing terms signify not autonomous places or things, but the abstracted "poles" of a tension that, as long as existence lasts, is indissoluble. Consequently, Voegelin insists that the fundamental choices we make in determining the meanings of our own existences involve the acceptance or the nonacceptance of the obligations and the opportunities we have been granted as intermediary presences. We may, at best, make a recurring effort to attune our understanding, feelings, and actions to the truths of transcendent being through following the urgings of reason, conscience, and grace, an attunement Voegelin is satisfied to describe as *movement* from "human imperfection toward the perfection of the divine ground that moves [one]."[7] Any notion of personal destiny, however, that derives from imagining a completion to this process, any image

---

6. Ibid., 90–91 (emphasis added); Voegelin, "Equivalences of Experience," 119.
7. *Anamnesis*, 103.

of "immortality gained," belongs to mythic elaboration. As such, Voegelin would hasten to emphasize, it performs a vital and salutary function in existential orientation. But no such image should be mistaken for a definitive answer to the question about the meaning or the outcome of any personal struggle within existence. No one can answer with certainty what one's future or ultimate relation to the being beyond perishing existence might be, any more than one might exhaustively explain why one has a role to play at all, or what meaning that role shall ultimately contribute to the drama of the Whole.

Thirdly, there is the mystery of history. The last chapter has explained the rudimentary facts that for Voegelin render the drama of history unknowable in its ultimate meaning. The most important of these facts is, again, that its origin and its promise are enveloped in a non-finite dimension of meaning. What is humanly knowable about the meaning of historical advance Voegelin summarizes by pointing to the parallels that can be drawn between the structure of personal existence and the structure of history. Just as the meaning of any individual's life is fashioned from a wide variety of possible responses to the presence of the ground, so the meaning of history has taken shape, and continues to take shape, from the entire manifold of human responses to the "tension toward eternal being." Those accumulated responses show patterns, and those patterns show direction: the direction Voegelin refers to in speaking of the "transfiguration" of reality, which proceeds through the advance to explicit knowledge of transcendence and the achievements of differentiating consciousness. Since this is the essence of history, it is the fact that itself ultimately wants explanation. In *The Ecumenic Age,* Voegelin has reduced this mystery of historical advance to three pointed questions:

(1) Why should there be epochs of advancing insight at all? why is the structure of reality not known in differentiated form at all times?

(2) Why must the insights be discovered by such rare individuals as prophets, philosophers, and saints? why is not every man the recipient of the insights?

(3) Why when the insights are gained, are they not generally accepted? why must the epochal truth go through the historical torment of imperfect articulation, evasion, skepticism, disbelief, rejection, deformation, and of renaissances, renovations, rediscoveries, rearticulations, and further differentiations?

These questions, of course, cannot be answered, nor are they meant to be—"on the contrary, they symbolize the mystery in the structure of history by their unanswerability."[8]

To be sure, Voegelin explains, there are philosophers who, moved by anxiety in the face of our ignorance about the ultimate meaning of historical process, reject its mysteriousness, attempting to "downgrade" its mystery to "a problem capable of resolution." Such efforts obviously require some kind of denial of transcendent meaning. This may take the form, he argues, of a speculative ascent of human insight to the divine perspective on history (as found, for example, in Hegel) or of the speculative reduction of historical processes to "world-immanent" events and entities (as found, for example, in Marx). As for himself, he asserts, he prefers to be "troubled" by the mystery of history.[9]

Fourthly, and briefly, there is the further mystery concerning the relation of individual destiny to the meaning of history as a whole. What relation does the process of historical development bear to the individual who may exist earlier or later in time? Voegelin has written little on this question, but enough to confirm that his philosophy of existence precludes any speculative reduction of individual to historical meaning. Personal existence is a participation in historical process, of course, but both are a participation in the unknowable ground. Personal meaning and historical meaning each tend toward fulfillment in the pole of reality beyond temporal and spatial conditions, but the relative autonomy of the personal relation to the ground cannot be dissolved into the meaning of the broader historical field within which it emerges. The distinction between their respective fulfillments is, from our human perspective, inviolable. "The relation between personal fulfilment and the partnership in the fulfilment of mankind is a mystery."[10]

These, then, are four true mysteries, Voegelin would say, because in each case a question of ultimate concern leads us to a meaning that is humanly unknowable, to a boundary where we are brought face to face

8. *The Ecumenic Age*, 316.
9. Voegelin, "History and Gnosis," 76. On this view of Hegel and Marx, see Voegelin, "On Hegel"; *The Ecumenic Age*, 254–69; *In Search of Order*, 48–70; *From Enlightenment to Revolution*, 240–302; and "Science, Politics, and Gnosticism," 23–28, 34–40, 64–80.
10. *The World of the Polis*, 4.

with the fact of transcendent meaning. These mysteries, however, raise further questions about existence and about the process of reality. And it is Voegelin's taking up of these further questions that constitutes one of his most impressive philosophical achievements. What is this further, secondary field of questions and corresponding mysteries?

In archaic or compact imagination, it will be recalled, the perfection of the ground is conceived in terms of cosmic entities and their relationships. The effort to order society and personal life is therefore conceived as a struggle within the cosmos, a cosmos that includes both the powers that create and preserve truth and harmony and the sources of imperfection and disorder. But when the differentiating insights separate the perfection of the ground from the physical universe, a shadow falls over the struggle for personal and social fulfillment, insofar as perfect attunement or reconciliation with what is most lasting in reality can no longer reasonably be conceived as possible under worldly conditions. The insights place the index of imperfection on the whole of finite reality. Consequently, the struggle for the realization of meaning, for fulfillment, shifts from being a thoroughly intracosmic conflict to involving, at its deepest level, a "movement," as Voegelin says, from the imperfection of the finite cosmos in the "direction" of the perfection of the transcendent ground. To our concern with the familiar struggle in the world's time between good and evil, order and disorder, is added the disturbing insight that the entire realm of existence in time is "disorder," insofar as we measure it by the transcendent order of its completed and perfected meaning. Inevitably, then, the noetic and pneumatic differentiations lead to a new kind of vision of the human struggle, a vision beyond the horizon of ancient mythic thinking, in which social and personal existence find fulfillment, not in this world, but in a Beyond of the world.

The presence of this sort of imaginative vision typifies what Voegelin calls "eschatological consciousness." In his estimation, any contemporary philosopher finds himself or herself confronted with problems that are simply unintelligible without a comprehension of the eschatological insights that underlie such imaginative visions—of the validity of those insights, of the philosophical problems they raise, of the passions they ignite, of the prophetic explanations and exhortations they engender, and, finally and not least significantly, of their susceptibility to misinterpretation in any number of manners. Voegelin has written on all of

these factors in contexts ranging from the first emergence of eschatological speculation in Hebraic prophetism to the emergence of the many
modern political variants of what he would describe as "immanentized"
eschatological visions—that is, visions that transmute the notion of a
transfigured reality beyond the present world into the notion of a new,
perfected realm of worldly existence, to succeed at some future date the
current, imperfect state of things.[11] But pertinent here is his position on
what contribution eschatological insights make to our confrontation
with mystery.

First of all, according to Voegelin, the insights themselves are valid.
The ground and its perfection truly do transcend the world proportionate to human comprehension, and this world is truly "moving" toward its
ground, ontologically, through the seeking and questioning, knowing
and loving, of human consciousness. And because the insights are valid,
the mystery of reality looms larger. New, unanswerable questions trou-
ble the questioner.

The most important of these is whether or not the world itself, with its
dangers and accidents, pain and sickness, injustice and unreason, poverty and hunger, war and death, reduced to the status of "disorder" in
comparison with the perfected meaning of its Beyond, ought not to be
considered an evil, a hindrance to the *nous* or *pneuma* in consciousness
that seeks the fullness of its own identity in transcendent being. Perhaps
the world itself, at least under its present conditions, is to be despised and
"overcome" as an obstacle to living in attunement with divine being;
perhaps this perishable human body is merely the "tomb" of an immortal spirit that will find true "life" only when it escapes into a Beyond of
the world; perhaps the world as it is revealed through our senses is an
illusion, to be transcended through meditation or other salvational procedures; perhaps, in the limit, the physical world is the creation of an evil
divinity, a world into which our spirits have strayed and out of which
they must find their way back to their proper abode. All of these concep-
tions are familiar to us from the texts and practices of the world's higher
religions and from strands in the Greek philosophical tradition. They

11. On the Hebrew origin of eschatological symbols, see especially *Israel and Revelation*, 302–3, 309–10, 343–45. For an account of Voegelin's theory of the "immanentization" of eschatological symbols, see *The New Science of Politics*, 107–32.

are, Voegelin would say, attempts to make sense of the "stratification" of reality and consciousness that results from the differentiation of transcendence. All of them are appealing, and not the least important reason for that appeal is the fact that, by placing the accent of evil on life under worldly conditions, the mysteries of disorder, of iniquity and suffering, are made somewhat less mysterious. The human role in the cosmic drama can be imagined to have the function of overcoming and escaping that evil and uniting wholly with the transcendent ground—or, in modern immanentist variations, of completely eliminating the sources of disorder and evil through science or education or a transformation of human nature, and so perfecting the world itself.

Voegelin has written on this attitude extensively under the general heading of "gnostic" solutions to the problems of eschatological consciousness. The conceit of ancient Gnostic sects was that the world is an alien place, created by an evil God, from which we may find a return to our true homeland through gaining the right knowledge (gnosis), whose use will assure our salvation. The general attitude contained in this view, Voegelin finds, is not a relic of antiquity. One of the most well-known features of Voegelin's work is his characterization of modernity in general, and of some of the most influential modern philosophies and political theories in particular, as gnostic in principle and in orientation. First brought to a wide audience in *The New Science of Politics,* Voegelin's argument is based on the following propositions: (1) the essential features of ancient gnosticism derive from a harsh dissatisfaction with the world, leading to belief that the world itself is wicked, that salvation from the evil of the world is possible, that such salvation is to be worked through human action, and that the means to salvific action is knowledge of the proper method; (2) salvation from the evil world may also be understood as "destruction of the old world and passage to the new"; and (3) modern movements such as "progressivism, positivism, Marxism, psychoanalysis, communism, fascism, and national socialism" all typify a "secular" gnostic attitude in that they offer salvation from an evil or botched order of reality to a new or perfected order of reality by means of one or another type of knowledge, through the promise of a transfiguration of *this* world. But since Voegelin understands the core of the gnostic attitude, ancient or modern, to be a rejection of reality as it is divinely given and a desire to re-create it after human liking, he sees it as a revolt against truth and reality, and, of course, as a doomed enterprise: "The gnostic's flight from a truly dreadful, confusing, and oppressive state of the world is understandable," but "the structure of the order of being will not change because one finds it defective and runs away from it."[12]

Indeed, when the question about the relationship between existence in the world and the fact of its ascertained Beyond is answered in the gnostic manner, there occurs, Voegelin tells us, a fundamental distortion in our interpretation of both reality as a whole and the demands of existence. It must be remembered that the transcendent ground is the formative origin of existing things; it is discovered in the search for the causes of this cosmos in which we live. It is, in fact, no other than the Intelligence that orders this intelligible universe, the Creator-God who creates this world in its entirety, the principle (Logos, Tao) that makes the things that exist to be what they are. "The discovery of the ground," Voegelin writes, "does not condemn the field of existent things to irrelevance but, on the contrary, establishes it as the reality that derives the meaning of its existence from the ground; and inversely, the [questioning search], as it ascends over the hierarchy of being, leads toward the ground because the ground is the origin of the hierarchy."[13] It follows that it is rationally impermissible to separate the transcendence revealed in human consciousness (the divine Beyond) from the originating power that forms and preserves all things (the divine Beginning). *And if the two are identical—if the ground is one—then participating in the conditions of existence cannot be, of its own accord, a state of alienation from the ground.* The imperfections of the cosmos, one might say, enjoy the sanction of divine perfection.

Admittedly, this does little to explain the mysteries of suffering and

---

12. Voegelin, "Ersatz Religion," 83; *The New Science of Politics*, 124; "Science, Politics and Gnosticism," 11–12. The standard text on ancient Gnosticism to which Voegelin refers is Hans Jonas, *The Gnostic Religion*. For Voegelin's interpretation of the gnostic attitude, ancient and modern, see *The New Science of Politics*, 107–89; and the essays in *Science, Politics, and Gnosticism*. His position has been amply criticized, and it should be mentioned that Voegelin came eventually to explain that his use of the category of "gnosticism" in these works, though justifiable, involved some oversimplification. In his late view, modernity is characterized by a secular blend of a variety of attitudes, the gnostic being but one, that have in common the desire for, and the claim to provide a method for, the transfiguration of an evil reality into a perfected one through human action. See "Philosophies of History," 136.

13. *The Ecumenic Age*, 324.

iniquity. In fact, it makes them all the more unsettling, not least because, with the one transcendent ground responsible for the cosmos and its structure, the unavoidable calamities of nature such as sickness, famine, early death, and so on must *not* be classified as intrinsically evil. And what about human iniquity, the moral and spiritual evils? In light of the differentiating insights, it can only be concluded that these arise from the human abuse of human freedom. That is, the differentiation of consciousness "requires a monistic symbolism for expressing the differentiating experience of a world- transcendent divine being," thus making it impossible, "within the logic of conversion," to render a second divinity, or any co-representation of the ground, responsible for moral and spiritual evils. But still, one may ponder, we humans did not create ourselves, did not grant ourselves the freedom we seem bound to abuse. What then is the meaning of our being formed as we are, destined, as it were, to bring discord into being? As can be seen, far from resolving perplexity over the meaning of either natural suffering or the human misuse of freedom, the differentiating insights, when kept in proper perspective, illuminate them as true mysteries—that is, as having an ultimate meaning we know to be humanly unknowable—by revealing the cosmic order that includes the human potential to abuse freedom to be an inextricable whole emergent from the one divine ground, for an ultimate purpose regarding which, as Plato has said, "we know nothing at all."[14]

This is one of the reasons why vilification of the temporal world—or of the untransformed world we inhabit—has always been and remains a popular response to the challenges posed by eschatological insight. As Voegelin points out, while such vilification distorts the truth, it also assuages the anxiety that, as long as the truth of transcendence is sensed, is aroused by the stark illumination of both the permanence of the miseries of existence and our permanent ignorance with respect to their ultimate meaning or value. It is hardly surprising, then, that the condemnation and devaluation of existence in this world has been a prominent feature in Western culture since the emergence of eschatological consciousness

---

14. *Israel and Revelation,* 50–51; Plato, *Laws* 644d–e. Plato's comment is a response to the question as to why the gods made human beings, whether as a plaything, or for some more serious purpose. I have used the translation of Voegelin's in "Wisdom," 337. See also Voegelin's discussion of this passage in "The Gospel and Culture," 185–88.

more than two millennia ago. Nevertheless, Voegelin insists that such attitudes can exercise a widespread influence only where there is also a widespread loss of what he calls "the balance of consciousness." This notion deserves some consideration.

The balance of consciousness is what might be called the primary virtue of differentiated consciousness. It consists in not letting the discovery, or the suspicion of the existence, of transcendent being disorient and frighten one in such a way that it leads one to devalue or reject either the immanent or the transcendent pole of being. In other words, one does not let the world as it is be degraded into "an untruth to be overcome by the truth of transfigured reality"; but neither is the fact and the perfection of transcendent being denied.[15] Rather, one accepts that the meaning of the finite cosmos is incomplete, but fittingly so, as well as that a transcendent fulfillment of that meaning is really discerned in human consciousness. And one accepts, therefore, the life of reason and spirit as that of mediating, of being intermediate between, the truths of finite and of transcendent being, and consequently one accepts also the task of understanding and sanctifying the conditions of finite existence that make it possible to fulfill this function.

It is obvious, looking over Voegelin's lifetime of work, that one of his most persistent concerns has been to advance the understanding of precisely those philosophical issues whose critical clarification serves to protect, and to promote, this balance of consciousness. His theory of consciousness is manifestly the centerpiece of that effort. Since the tension of existence bridges, as it were, the finite cosmos and its non-finite ground, the function of conscious existence is certainly not to escape or condemn the former in the name of the latter. Existence *is* the tension, it *is* the action of bridging. If one grasps the fundamental validity of the differentiating insights and their eschatological promise, and if at the same time one doesn't lose one's bearings amid the hypostatic imagery of two realms or worlds, one will be able in Voegelin's opinion to realize that the primary duty of conscious existence, in a culture informed by the differentiating experiences, is to honor participatory tension itself. To know of transcendent meaning, and to struggle for existential order by allowing one's character to be formed by rational or spiritual truths of transcen-

15. *The Ecumenic Age,* 228.

dent validity while loving, and not rejecting, the world in which the struggle occurs, is the activity that, in Voegelin's view, "saves" differentiated existence from meaninglessness and loss.[16]

Finally, now, it is this struggle for existential order in light of the knowledge of transcendent being that for Voegelin raises the most radical question of all concerning the overall structure of the process of reality. Why, he asks, has the one divine ground formed a finite cosmos that includes the human questioner, only to require that questioner to seek, in resistance to existential ignorance and disorder, the ground itself beyond the finite cosmos, and find his or her "salvation" in increasing degrees of participatory attunement with its truth? This question has been touched upon already in the second chapter, in the discussion of Voegelin's question about why a cosmos formed from its divine Beginning should be moving, in a transfigurative process whose medium is human consciousness, toward a divine Beyond of itself. The human struggle represents a conflict in the very structure of being. In mythic terms, this is a conflict "between a God of the Beyond who orders the psyche of man by attracting it toward Himself and a God of the Beginning who creates an order so imperfect that it requires a special effort of revelation and response to extract man from the disorder of reality." Why is the struggle necessary? This is a question that, once asked, expands immediately to encompass the mysteries of personal destiny and of history. Why is the human "transfiguring" response only partially successful? As Voegelin comments, "[T]he fulfillment of human nature emerges against the background of the mystery of its failure." And why is there a historical process of discovery concerning these truths? "Why is the structure of reality not known in differentiated form at all times?" These already discussed questions and the mysteries they illuminate take their place in the embracing context of the mystery of the divine purpose in creating a creature who is required to seek for a "saving" participation in a Beyond of creation in order to suffer meaningfully the toils of creaturely existence.[17]

It is apparent that all of these mysteries form an interlocking network

16. For Voegelin's interpretation of the symbol of "salvation" as used in Plato's dialogues and in the New Testament writings, and for his comparison of its use in these two contexts, see "The Gospel and Culture," 179–88; and "Wisdom," 365–71.

17. "The Beginning and the Beyond," 211; *Plato and Aristotle*, 358; *The Ecumenic Age*, 316.

of insights. It is not going too far to say that the entire complex, as an interpretation of the human situation, stands or falls together. There is no mystery of transfiguration in which the spatiotemporal universe is dynamically engaged, through human consciousness, in transcending its meaning toward a more eminent degree of meaning than it presently incarnates unless there is such a transcendent meaning. Likewise, there is no mystery of personal destiny, or of history, unless we are really participants in a process whose higher meaning we are incapable of penetrating because it transcends what can be humanly known. In short, Voegelin's entire analysis of mystery—and, by implication, of human existence—depends upon the validity of his theory of the differentiation of transcendence; consequently, it will appear cogent only to that reader who is ready to affirm the insights that underlie that theory. Such affirmation, in turn, can only result from a willingness to ask the question of the ground and to discover that, in fact, it is reasonable to judge the ground of being to be nothing conditioned or contingent, nothing in space and time. In other words, the two preconditions for such affirmation are: the question of the ground must be asked; and the questioner must not be satisfied with an answer that falls short of the recognition of transcendent meaning. The latter precondition is likely, however, to go unfulfilled on the part of the contemporary reader, for many reasons, but the following are three of the most obvious:

(1) What Voegelin calls the differentiation of consciousness is existentially demanding and intellectually challenging. Not everyone is up to that demand or that challenge.

(2) For those who suspect, surmise, or accept the truth of the transcendence of the ground, there is still the problem of coping with its mystery, of finding the love, hope, and faith that enable one to face and continually be delivered from, as Kierkegaard would say, the anxiety its uncertainties produce. Not everyone can summon or develop the requisite "virtues of existential tension." "The 'balance of consciousness' [achieved by those who can] face the Mystery is a rare event indeed, carefully to be preserved as a strand in Western civilization. . . . To face the Mystery of Reality means to live in the faith that is the substance of things hoped for and the proof of things unseen (Heb. 11:1)."[18]

18. *The Ecumenic Age,* 329.

(3) Perhaps most importantly, the contemporary Westerner is at a disadvantage due to centuries of cultural conditioning in which the question of the ground has been answered by so-called "scientific" interpretations of reality, which, as already discussed, identify one or another type of finite structure, or principle of relation among finite structures, as the most real or lasting dimension of being, and reject any notion of non-spatiotemporally conditioned being as superstitious. The degree of authority these interpretations presently enjoy scarcely needs mentioning. There is much in the contemporary "climate of opinion," to use Whitehead's phrase, that encourages the questioner to be satisfied with something in the "immanent realm of being" when asking about the ground.

It remains, nonetheless, that such "immanentizing" answers are ultimately unintelligible, from Voegelin's position. They are so because the intentional range of the question of the ground, *as a question,* is wider than the horizon of any possible human understanding. In the noetic and pneumatic differentiations, the human Question, the desire to know, finds the Mystery that is its correlative. And in the last analysis there "is no answer to the Question other than the Mystery as it becomes luminous in the acts of questioning." Since consciousness can out-question the knowable, out-question what is conditioned by space and time, by so doing it is questioning itself, and not any conceivable answer, that "becomes the criterion of the truth [of the ground] truly found."[19] Again, this simply makes explicit, for differentiated consciousness, what is implicit in the compact experience of the ground, which feels existence to be derived from and embraced by the inscrutable, encompassing power of "the gods." When the question of the ground is presumed to be answerable, within the reach of finite intelligence, then in a very real sense it is no longer the question of the ground at all. And when the true question of the ground is thus eclipsed, the result is a disturbance in consciousness.

Voegelin has underscored all this by writing that the mystery of the process of reality is "a dimension of consciousness itself." In this statement he appears to be conjoining the awareness of mystery with that "structural dimension" of consciousness he refers to as "luminosity" in *In Search of Order.* This is the awareness of one's own consciousness as an

19. Ibid., 330; "The Beginning and the Beyond," 176.

event in Being and of one's consubstantiality with the Whole. For the ancients, who experienced the ultimate powers of being in the immediacy of nature, for whom nature was a "Thou" and "the gods" palpable presences, this sense of consubstantiality, of common participation, was inescapable. Ancient mythic consciousness, as Voegelin says, was characterized by "the *predominance* of the experience of participation." Consequently, a sense of the mystery of things, the mystery of origins and the encompassing unknown, was guaranteed. But this is not so following the impact of the differentiations of consciousness. When one's cultural and linguistic ambience has been shaped for centuries by the liberation of "nature" from the divine ground and by the vision of a created world that is in no wise to be confused with its Creator, then the ground, as one might put it, is harder to find. One could say that the dimension of luminosity in consciousness, of belonging to Being, tends to weaken because the images and symbols that can convincingly mediate a sense of common reality, of the ground, refer to transcendent reality—and one must have attained to the level of the differentiating insights in order for them to evoke an experience of ultimate participation, of "luminous" belonging. And for the contemporary Westerner, the situation is even less conducive to such experiences, due to the impact of modern science. The spellbinding successes of the modern physical sciences, beginning in the sixteenth century, have encouraged their methods to be adopted as the sole criteria for determining what is real and what is true, and this in turn has given rise to widespread popular acceptance, in our own day, of interpretations of reality that systematically exclude whatever cannot be physically explored and verified. From Voegelin's point of view, as has been mentioned, this is a latter-day version of compact consciousness but one that, unlike the archaic, excludes the ground ("the gods") from its "catalogue of items" that make up reality. Cultural conditions have conspired to foster, as he puts it, "the vulgarian belief that man is no longer living in a cosmos but in a 'physical universe'"; and they furthermore have fostered, in the name of "science," an attitude of suspicion and skepticism with regard to all religious and metaphysical questions, or specifically, questions that go beyond the field of what is known to be verifiable by physical experiment, not to speak of questions that point beyond what is known to be knowable. In such a climate, Voegelin explains, the obstacles to effective mediation of the ground as transcendence are extensive enough that the dimension of "luminosity" can atrophy, be forgotten or repressed, to the extent that the ground and its mystery become "excluded from consciousness," relegated to the "unconscious." Voegelin has much to say about the personal and political repercussions, including "mental disturbances" and "pneumopathological" states, of such a condition of "imbalanced, fragmentized consciousness," which he considers epidemic in the modern West. But the central point to be made here is that the question of the ground is always, by definition, oriented toward mystery—and, since this question is what we *are,* since consciousness is precisely a "tension toward the ground," the loss of ability to experience our participation in the Mystery of Reality is a loss of ourselves.[20]

Voegelin's insistence upon the truth of the mysteries of existence, as part of his more comprehensive analysis of existence and history, must therefore be understood first and foremost as a philosopher's effort to open the way for his readers to an experience of participating in divine reality. To that purpose, he continually adverts to the centrality of the question of the ground, while frequently pointing out the distortion or eclipse it suffers when it is presumed to be a question capable of being given a definitive answer. To invoke its proper intelligibility, he at times refers to the famous two sentences of Leibniz that, as he says, have reduced the question to a "brilliant starkness": Why is there something; why not nothing? And why do things exist as they do, and not otherwise? Obviously such questions cannot be answered with "verifiable statements." No theory and no science can ever explain, in an ultimate sense, why a structured reality exists, or why it is these structures, and not others, that have emerged or evolved. "The epiphany of structures in reality—be they atoms, molecules, genes, biological species, races, human consciousness, or language—is a mystery inaccessible to explanation." One can respond, of course, as Leibniz did, that the proper answer to these questions is "God"; but that answer, as should be obvious

20. "Wisdom," 372–73; *Israel and Revelation,* 3 (emphasis added); *The Ecumenic Age,* 203; *In Search of Order,* 59–60. For an introduction to what Voegelin means by "mental disturbance" and "pneumopathology" in connection with existential closure toward the ground and its mystery, see *Anamnesis,* 97–103.

by now, is itself a question in that it evokes every one of the previously discussed mysteries. Voegelin would insist that the primary function of such questions is not to push us toward conclusive answers, but to "keep open one's human condition" by reminding the questioner that being human means to search for the meaning of being human.[21]

Mythos and Vision

A good deal has already been said in previous chapters about Voegelin's understanding of the nature and function of myths. His most important thesis is that mythoi, as imaginative answers to questions about the meaning of the Whole, have not become unnecessary as a result of philosophical or scientific discoveries about reality. The ancient myths, founded upon "intracosmic" experiences of the ground, became incredible, of course, in the wake of the rise of rational-critical thought. But unfortunately, from Voegelin's point of view, those members of the cultural elite in ancient Greece who boldly rejected not only the traditional myths about "the gods" but also the very fact of divinity itself set the pattern for "enlightened" generations to come, down to the present. Their mistake, Voegelin would say, is to suppose that the discovery that the finite universe can be explained in terms of structural regularities and impersonal forces—the discovery of "nature"—dissolves the mystery of formative origins along with its sacred character. It scarcely needs to be emphasized how this supposition has been reinforced by the modern scientific revolution and its legacy, or how that revolution has prompted, beginning with the ferocity of the Enlightenment philosophes, a devaluation and debunking of mythic representation that has enjoyed great social success and permeates our contemporary milieu. Voegelin, of course, is not the only thinker in this century who perceives this wholesale denigration of mythic expression as unhealthy; critical reappraisal of the myth, in all its varieties and degrees of sophistication, and recognition of its basic validity and central function in human self-understanding, are hallmarks of influential streams of twentieth-century thought. But Voegelin's theory

21. *The Ecumenic Age*, 74; Voegelin, "Questions Up," 103; *In Search of Order*, 17; "In Search of the Ground," 3.

of consciousness, in conjunction with his vast acquaintance with source materials, allows him to interpret both the career of the myth in the West and the crucial role myth plays in conscious activity in a way that is perhaps uniquely informative.

Voegelin would approve Stanley Rosen's description that "myth re-collects the fragments of man's intermediate existence into the unity of the beginning and the end." For Voegelin, the most obvious fact about human existence is its "intermediate" status. Limitation is of the essence of our being: we are human because we have a restricted understanding. Understanding our own restrictions, however, we understand there is a fullness of understanding we lack; aware of our separate, intermediate existences, we are aware of a fullness of reality in which we participate. To long for that fullness of understanding and for fuller participation in being is the dynamic core of our existence, according to Voegelin—and therefore, to understand the meaning of our separate existences *by understanding the unity of the Whole to which we belong* is an unvarying human concern. Myth, for Voegelin, is the "adequate and exact . . . instrument of expression" for articulating and communicating insights into the meaning of the process of reality as a Whole, because (1) the myth does not claim to be a definitive account—it is a "likely story" that accords with the present state of our knowledge about reality and human nature—and so does not violate our awareness of the limitations of human perspective and (2) the myth tells a story that makes sense of our experiences of purpose and struggle, risk and failure, desire and achievement. In short, it unites the individual and social dramas of our lives within a supervening drama of being. While the ancient myth performed these tasks uncritically, the discovery of the transcendence of the ground has induced a critical awareness that all mythic representation involves the interpretation of the unknown by analogy with the known. And new mythoi have appeared, for example in Plato's dialogues and in the Gospels, that reflect the advances in human self-understanding occasioned by the differentiating insights. There could, perhaps, be yet further adjustments of mythoi in accordance with further advances of insight into personal and historical meaning; but there can never be a replacement of mythoi by definitive knowledge, nor the absence of the human need to fashion an understanding of the supervening context of meaning within which our lives begin and end "in the middle of the story." The "likely truth" of the myth, which begins and completes the story we know ourselves to be acting in, is the *only* symbolic vehicle we have to consciously unite our lives with the divine unity from which we have emerged—or "fallen"—into separate existence.[22]

If the above summary alone were the substance of Voegelin's analysis of myth, however, it would not be particularly unique. Its profounder dimension is provided by the explanation of mythic symbolism in light of Voegelin's theory of consciousness.

One may recall Voegelin's insistence, from the beginning of his philosophical career, that consciousness, while experienced as individual, also belongs, and is conscious of belonging, to the process of reality within which it occurs. Human consciousness is an event within Being, an illumination "within" reality; as Voegelin puts it in *In Search of Order,* consciousness is "luminous" as well as "intentional." Now the function of the mythopoet (and the artist), as Voegelin sees it, is to attend to this latter dimension of consciousness, to nourish its sense of consubstantiality, and to suffer, in the desire to represent the truths about the unity of the Whole, to be "spoken through" so that the story reality is trying to tell is glimpsed in appropriate images and symbols. What we respond to in the truly telling mythos (and in the convincing work of art) is not the inventive personality who fashions analogies with facility and discretion in order to show forth the unknown; we respond to the authority of reality itself, moving us to the depths, as we recognize a revelatory authenticity in the complexes of images or the events of the narrative. The compelling myth, arising from the "depths" of Being, is, Voegelin would say, both human and divine. "This consciousness of the Beyond of consciousness which constitutes consciousness by reaching into it, is the area of reality which articulates itself through the symbols of mythic imagination."[23]

Now, beginning with *The Ecumenic Age,* but increasingly in his major works after it, Voegelin employs the word *vision,* drawn from Plato's use of the term *opsis,* as a technical category to signify precisely these

22. Rosen, *Plato's Symposium,* 1; *From Enlightenment to Revolution,* 22; *In Search of Order,* 27–28. On the transition from uncritical to critical appreciation of the myth, see *Israel and Revolution,* 5.

23. "The Gospel and Culture," 188. On the relation between art and cosmological consciousness, see "In Search of the Ground," 22.

"human-divine symbols of mythical imagination." "The 'vision' is not somebody's fancy but the imaginative power of response to the reality seen; and the reality seen is the cause (*aition*) of this power (*dynamis*)." Therefore, it is inappropriate, he says, to speak of the "subject" or "object" of the vision; to split subject and object asunder would, in this case, obliterate the specific meaning of the cognitive event, which involves the participational identity between the reality that constitutes consciousness and the human consciousness imagining reality. Vision, one might say, is the symbolic expression of meaning correlative to the experience of mystery insofar as, in Marcel's description, it is "a sphere where the distinction between what is in me and what is before me loses its meaning and its initial validity." As Voegelin puts it, the language of the vision "does not merely refer to reality but is reality itself emerging as the luminous 'word' from the divine-human encounter." And again: "The vision emerges as a symbol from the Metaxy, and the symbol is both human and divine. Any attempt to break up the mystery of divine-human participation, as it occurs in a theophanic event [which gives rise to visionary symbols], is fatuous."[24]

One advantage of the term, significant from the point of view of Voegelin's attempt to develop a truly adequate theory of consciousness, is that it gives him a theoretical category to refer specifically to the cognitional activity comprising every genuine mythopoeic response to the mystery of luminous participation. Although he nowhere spells the fact out clearly, Voegelin appears to have adopted "vision" as a differentiated philosophical category referring to a specific capacity or structure in consciousness, like the structures of intentionality and luminosity and the overall structure of consciousness as a *metaxy*. These structures are able to be distinguished, of course, through the additional capacity of "reflective distance," which enables consciousness to grasp and articulate its own nature. *Vision* would therefore be what Voegelin calls, in *In Search of Order*, a "reflective symbol," specifically the symbol that in his later work heuristically identifies all acts of imaginative experience and expression that convincingly establish for a person, a people, or a tradition, a super-

24. Marcel, *Being and Having*, 117; Voegelin, "The Beginning and the Beyond," 229, 231; *The Ecumenic Age*, 243. Voegelin identifies *Timaeus* 47 and *Republic* 507–9 as the passages from which he has drawn his interpretation of Plato's use of the term *opsis*.

vening context of meaning regarding the participation of conscious existence in the Whole of reality.

Some final conclusions may now be drawn by stating that if we in contemporary culture let our questions of ultimate concern carry us on to the recognition of the mysteries of transcendent meaning, we shall require appropriate and compelling visions or mythoi in order to properly order our lives. We shall require them to help us keep our bearings amid the "transcendental border problems" as we try to appropriate the significance of our transfiguring participation in non-spatiotemporal being. Voegelin's comments concerning the compatibility of the "Pauline myth" with the mysteries of transcendent origins, personal destiny, and history have been noted. But a guiding, informing vision of the Whole congruent with insight into transcendent mystery need not be either so differentiated or so complex—indeed, at the most rudimentary level of effectiveness, it need only mediate the fact of the transcendence of the ground, the fact of a supervening story, and the "likeliness" of the symbolic tale. Such a rudimentary vision is expressed, for example, in the single word *God*. *God* is a mythopoeic symbol arising from discernment of the transcendent pole of the participatory tension of existence that, through a single word or image, evokes "the mystery that lets all meaningfully structured stories within the process [of reality] be experienced as substories of [a] comprehending story."[25]

Of course, language about "God," or any other mythopoesis concerning the mystery of the ground, may be "misconstrued as a conceptual language referring to a divine entity."[26] Such literalizing misinterpretations of imaginative visions conspire to hinder the effective mediation of the true mysteries, to the limit of rendering ridiculous, to the enlightened Westerner, the notion of transcendent being. And when, in the modern West, access to transcendence is lost, and the mystery of the ground "forgotten," the stage is set for interpretations of the Whole that exclude the sacred dimension altogether.

Now, in Voegelin's estimation, the presence of some kind of imaginative representation of the meaning of the whole process of reality, providing an ultimate meaning-context for human living, is a constant in the

---

25. *The World of the Polis*, 137; *In Search of Order*, 82.
26. *In Search of Order*, 68.

structure of consciousness. There is no "overcoming," as he says, of the myth; there is only the choice between more or less appropriate, or more or less inappropriate, mythoi of the Whole. One characteristic of modernity, he would say, is the widespread acceptance of "stories"—such as those of scientific or philosophical materialism, or of certain streams of political revolutionary imagination—that eliminate the divinely constitutive dimension from the reality envisioned. In other words, whatever the ground of reality is assumed, however inchoatively, to be in such stories, it is not considered *the ground of consciousness* in such a way that it shares creative responsibility for "the imagery of expressive symbols" that interprets the comprehensive context of meaning. The "story" is therefore considered to be a purely human discovery, derived from purely human faculties of imagination and understanding. Such mythoi are, in Voegelin's view, "deformed" in principle, because they ignore the participatory dimension of consciousness; the "creatively formative force" of human imagination "is exposed to deformative perversion, [because] the creative partner imagines himself to be the sole creator of truth." Any story of the Whole that fails to acknowledge that the story itself has its origins in a more-than-human ground of consciousness that is ultimately mysterious is a false story; it is a deformed mythos that mistakes itself for logos.[27]

The appeal of such stories that exclude the sacred dimension of reality is not difficult to fathom. When the creative-imaginative power of the ground is eclipsed by the power of human imagination—when we "out-imagine" reality, as Voegelin says, and assume that we are the sole creators of truth—then we can dismiss as senseless those questions about the ground that, by reminding us that our own consciousnesses are ontologically derivative events, lead us to recognize our existential involvement in mysteries beyond our full comprehension. And with the dismissal of those questions we can indulge in the comfort provided by supposing that our stories of the Whole are exactly and definitively true, that our perspective on reality exceeds that of "intermediary" existence, and in fact can encompass the meaning of the process of reality from beginning to end. The attraction of allaying our anxieties about the meaning of our own search for meaning by "discovering" a story that is no

27. *Plato and Aristotle*, 187; *In Search of Order*, 37–38.

longer a likely mythos but a certain truth is so seductive, Voegelin would say, that it can prompt us to forget that "conscious existence is an event within reality," and that, in spite of all, we are "quite conscious of being constituted by the reality of which [we are] conscious."[28]

The criteria for determining what are appropriate mythoi of the Whole, Voegelin's analysis indicates, are established by nothing other than the questioning process itself, by the desire to know as it hearkens to each further relevant question concerning the meaning of existence. The question of the ground, sincerely asked, first of all insures the openness of consciousness to its status as created, and then as a seeker of the deeper meaning of the ground in which its own and all of finite reality participates. The transcendent meaning of that ground of all things, and the mysteries of personal destiny and history, are further facts that persistent and perspicacious questioning reveals. And then when recognized, Voegelin argues, all of these facts can only receive their full due in the conscious embrace of imaginative symbols that mediate the likely meaning of the comprehensive process in which we find ourselves. This, his writings persuade us, is the only way that we who are heirs to the legacy of the differentiation of transcendent meaning in the West can "forge a connection" with our own origins.

Voegelin's work, like that of Søren Kierkegaard, was written as a corrective to the spirit of the age. But perhaps even Kierkegaard did not perceive his society and his time in as harsh a light as Voegelin portrays modernity. His writings are possibly the most impassioned and virulent condemnation of modern Western culture that can be accredited to a philosophically competent scholar. Repeatedly he sums up the character of the last three centuries in the West as a "grotesque," an "imbecility," a "madhouse," in which intellectual life and political direction have alike lost their bearings to an unheard of degree. He in no way denies the importance or value of the tide of scientific discoveries, technological inventions, historical knowledge, and ardor of research and enterprise that have led the modern West to world dominance and to the unassailable perception of itself as civilization par excellence. But his assessment of what has been lost along with what has been gained leads him, in his

28. *In Search of Order*, 39; *Anamnesis*, 11.

most dolorous moment, to pronounce, simply, that the "death of the spirit is the price of progress." This, he exclaims, is the "mystery of the Western apocalypse."[29]

"Death of the spirit" may be translated, in the language of Voegelin's theory of consciousness, as widespread existential closure to the transcendent measure of reality. At the core of this closure is the inability or refusal of consciousness to attend to the first fact of its existence, which is that it suffers participation in the process of reality and that its own creative powers are derived. It is the curtailing of the desire to hearken to the ultimately constitutive ground that transcends human knowledge and control, and of the desire to acknowledge and respond, lovingly and creatively, to its mysterious dispensation. Voegelin is well aware of the difficulties involved in attributing causes, and in gauging responsibility, with regard to such epic developments. One finds that the tone of his writings, when he speaks of the "disorder" of modernity, oscillates between that of the angry prophet who is peculiarly sensitive to anything, even banal pastimes, that suggests rebellion against the divine measure of truth and existence, and that of the spiritual physician profoundly sympathetic to all those who, to his mind, are victims of the widespread "eclipse" of divine reality in Western culture. Closure to the ground is, in Voegelin's view, a form of disease, some of whose proximate causes can be diagnosed. One cause is the dissociation of traditional religious and philosophical symbols from their bases in concrete, recognizable experiences—a consequence in part of the "dogmatic hardening" of symbolic formulations, which has had the effect of rendering the "truth" a dead letter for many. Another is the impact and massive prestige of the mathematical and physical sciences, which have tended to make the nonphysical dimension of reality addressed by such symbols incredible. Yet another is the insistence on the possibility and need for complete certainty in the understanding of all facets of reality. Voegelin's mystagogy is a therapy directed against all of these causes of modern closure to transcendent reality. As he might put it: to personally recover the question of the ground at the heart of the tension of consciousness, and to preserve its "openness" to the mystery of its own origin and goal, is a process that alerts one to the futility and danger of claims to knowledge

29. *The New Science of Politics,* 131.

of absolute truth; and since to recover the Mystery of the Whole is to recover the mystery in all things, it is a process that also appropriately undermines the promise of total cognitive (and perhaps, in time, manipulative) mastery over personal, social, and historical processes.

It is Voegelin's philosophy of consciousness that underlies and justifies his therapeutic efforts. Its single greatest strength is that, through its "exegetic, not descriptive" language of "tension," "ground," "poles," and "*metaxy,*" it steadily subverts the tendency to conceive of the conscious subject as a type of Cartesian entity set over against a "world." Consciousness is *within* Being, is a participation in which the process of reality comes to reflective self-awareness. Apart from Heidegger, no modern philosopher besides Voegelin has worked so hard to deconstruct in a responsible and convincing way what might be called the anthropology of confrontation, in which consciousness and world remain in fixed alienation as the subject and object of finite being. Heidegger's analysis of Dasein as a "clearing in Being" is equivalent to Voegelin's analysis of consciousness as a "tension toward the ground" and a "luminous participation," insofar as both thinkers establish as a theoretical axis the participatory identity of conscious being and Being. But of the two it is Voegelin who has provided, not only the more satisfactory philosophical anthropology, but also a detailed philosophy of history consistent with understanding the primary fact of conscious existence to be participation in the Mystery of the Whole.

BIBLIOGRAPHY

The first part of this bibliography is made up of works by Voegelin used in this study, a selection consisting almost entirely of later writings and those in English. The second part is made up of other works consulted. For more comprehensive bibliographies of Voegelin's works, one should refer to those in Sandoz, *The Voegelinian Revolution,* and Cooper, *The Political Theory of Eric Voegelin.*

Works by Eric Voegelin

Anamnesis. Translated and edited by Gerhart Niemeyer. Notre Dame: University of Notre Dame Press, 1978.

Anamnesis: Zur Theorie der Geschichte und Politik. Munich: R. Piper and Co., 1966.

Autobiographical Reflections. Edited by Ellis Sandoz. Baton Rouge: Louisiana State University Press, 1989.

"Autobiographical Statement at Age Eighty-Two." In *The Beginning and the Beyond,* edited by Frederick Lawrence, 111–31. Chico, Calif.: Scholars Press, 1984.

"The Beginning and the Beyond: A Meditation on Truth." In *What Is History? And Other Late Unpublished Writings,* 173–232. Vol. 28 of *The Collected Works.* Baton Rouge: Louisiana State University Press, 1990.

The Collected Works of Eric Voegelin. 3 vols. to date. Vol. 12, *Published Essays, 1966–1985,* edited by Ellis Sandoz; Vol. 28, *What Is History? And Other Late Unpublished Writings,* edited by Thomas A. Hollweck and Paul Caringella. Baton Rouge: Louisiana State University Press, 1990.

"Configurations of History." In *Published Essays, 1966–1985,* 95–114. Vol. 12 of *The Collected Works.* Baton Rouge: Louisiana State University Press, 1990.

"Consciousness and Order: Foreword to 'Anamnesis' (1966)." Translation, by the author, of the "Vorwort" to *Anamnesis: Zur Theorie der Geschichte und Politik.* In *The Beginning and the Beyond,* edited by Frederick Lawrence, 35–41. Chico, Calif.: Scholars Press, 1984.

Conversations with Eric Voegelin. Edited by R. Eric O'Connor. Thomas More Institute Papers/76. Montreal: Perry Printing Limited, 1980.

"The Eclipse of Reality." In *Phenomenology and Social Reality,* edited by Maurice Natanson, 185–94. The Hague: Martinus Nijhoff, 1970.

"Epilogue." In *Eric Voegelin's Thought: A Critical Appraisal,* edited by Ellis Sandoz, 199–202. Durham, N.C.: Duke University Press, 1982.

"Equivalences of Experience and Symbolization in History." In *Published Essays, 1966–1985,* 115–33. Vol. 12 of *The Collected Works.* Baton Rouge: Louisiana State University Press, 1990.

"Ersatz Religion." In *Science, Politics, and Gnosticism.* Chicago: Henry Regnery Co., 1968.

From Enlightenment to Revolution. Edited by John H. Hallowell. Durham, N.C.: Duke University Press, 1975.

"The Gospel and Culture." In *Published Essays, 1966–1985,* 172–212. Vol. 12 of *The Collected Works.* Baton Rouge: Louisiana State University Press, 1990.

"History and Gnosis." In *The Old Testament and Christian Faith,* edited by Bernhard Anderson, 64–89. New York: Herder and Herder, 1969.

"Immortality: Experience and Symbol." In *Published Essays, 1966–1985,* 52–94. Vol. 12 of *The Collected Works.* Baton Rouge: Louisiana State University Press, 1990.

"In Search of the Ground." In *Conversations with Eric Voegelin,* edited by R. Eric O'Connor, 1–35. Thomas More Institute Papers/76. Montreal: Perry Printing Limited, 1980.

"The Meditative Origin of the Philosophical Knowledge of Order." Translation by Frederick Lawrence of "Der meditative Ursprung philosophischen Ordnungwissens." In *The Beginning and the Beyond,* edited by Frederick Lawrence, 43–51. Chico, Calif.: Scholars Press, 1984.

"Myth as Environment." In *Conversations with Eric Voegelin,* edited by R. Eric O'Connor, 113–54. Thomas More Institute Papers/76. Montreal: Perry Printing Limited, 1980.

The New Science of Politics. Chicago: University of Chicago Press, 1952.

"On Classical Studies." In *Published Essays, 1966–1985,* 256–64. Vol. 12 of *The Collected Works.* Baton Rouge: Louisiana State University Press, 1990.

"On Debate and Existence." In *Published Essays, 1966–1985,* 36–51. Vol. 12 of *The Collected Works.* Baton Rouge: Louisiana State University Press, 1990.

"On Hegel: A Study in Sorcery." In *Published Essays, 1966–1985,* 213–55. Vol. 12 of *The Collected Works.* Baton Rouge: Louisiana State University Press, 1990.

Order and History. 5 vols. Vol. 1, *Israel and Revelation,* 1956; Vol. 2, *The World of the Polis,* 1957; Vol. 3, *Plato and Aristotle,* 1957; Vol. 4, *The Ecumenic Age,* 1974; Vol. 5, *In Search of Order,* 1987. Baton Rouge: Louisiana State University Press.

"The Origins of Scientism." *Social Research* 15 (1948): 462–94.

"Philosophies of History: An Interview with Eric Voegelin." *New Orleans Review,* no. 2 (1973): 135–39.

"Political Theory and the Pattern of General History." *American Political Science Review* 38 (1944): 746–54.

"Questions Up." In *Conversations with Eric Voegelin,* edited by R. Eric O'Connor, 75–111. Thomas More Institute Papers/76. Montreal: Perry Printing Limited, 1980.

"Quod Deus Dicitur." In *Published Essays, 1966–1985,* 376–94. Vol. 12 of *The Collected Works.* Baton Rouge: Louisiana State University Press, 1990.

"Reason: The Classic Experience." In *Published Essays, 1966–1985,* 265–91. Vol. 12 of *The Collected Works.* Baton Rouge: Louisiana State University Press, 1990.

"Remembrance of Things Past." Chap. 1 of *Anamnesis.* Translated and edited by Gerhart Niemeyer. Notre Dame: University of Notre Dame Press, 1978. Reprinted in *Published Essays, 1966–1985,* 304–14. Vol. 12 of *The Collected Works.* Baton Rouge: Louisiana State University Press, 1990.

"Response to Professor Altizer's 'A New History and a New but Ancient God?'" In *Published Essays, 1966–1985,* 292–303. Vol. 12 of *The Collected Works.* Baton Rouge: Louisiana State University Press, 1990.

Science, Politics, and Gnosticism. Chicago: Henry Regnery Co., 1968.

"Science, Politics, and Gnosticism." Translated by William J. Fitzpatrick. In *Science, Politics, and Gnosticism.* Chicago: Henry Regnery Co., 1968.

"Theology Confronting World Religions?" In *Conversations with Eric Voegelin,* edited by R. Eric O'Connor, 37–74. Thomas More Institute Papers/76. Montreal: Perry Printing Limited, 1980.

"Toynbee's History as a Search for Truth." In *The Intent of Toynbee's History,* edited by Edward T. Gargan, 182–98. Chicago: Loyola University Press, 1961.

"Two Letters to Alfred Schuetz." In *The Philosophy of Order: Essays on History, Consciousness, and Politics,* edited by Peter J. Opitz and Gregor Sebba, 449–65. Stuttgart: Klett-Cotta, 1981.

"Wisdom and the Magic of the Extreme: A Meditation." In *Published Essays, 1966–1985,* 315–75. Vol. 12 of *The Collected Works.* Baton Rouge: Louisiana State University Press, 1990.

Other Works Consulted

Altizer, Thomas J. J. "A New History and a New but Ancient God? Voegelin's *The Ecumenic Age.*" In *Eric Voegelin's Thought: A Critical Appraisal,* edited by Ellis Sandoz, 179–88. Durham, N.C.: Duke University Press, 1982.

Anastaplo, George. "On How Eric Voegelin Has Read Plato and Aristotle." *Independent Journal of Philosophy* 5–6 (1988): 85–91.

Anderson, Bernhard W. "Politics and the Transcendent: Voegelin's Philosophical and Theological Exposition of the Old Testament in the Context of the Ancient Near East." In *Eric Voegelin's Search for Order in History,* edited by Stephen A. McKnight, 62–100. Baton Rouge: Louisiana State University Press, 1978.

Annice, Sister M., C.S.C. "Historical Sketch of the Theory of Participation." *New Scholasticism* 26 (1952): 49–79.

Aristotle. *Aristotle's Metaphysics.* Translated by Hippocrates G. Apostle. Grinnell, Iowa: The Peripatetic Press, 1979.

———. *Aristotle's Physics.* Translated by Hippocrates G. Apostle. Grinnell, Iowa: The Peripatetic Press, 1980.

———. *The Basic Works of Aristotle.* Edited by Richard McKeon. New York: Random House, 1941.

———. *Nicomachean Ethics.* Translated by Martin Ostwald. Indianapolis: The Bobbs-Merrill Company, 1983.

Augustine, Saint. *Confessions.* Translated by R. S. Pine-Coffin. Baltimore: Penguin Books, 1984.

Baynes, Kenneth, James Bohman, and Thomas McCarthy, eds. *After Philosophy: End or Transformation?* Cambridge: The MIT Press, 1989.

Bergson, Henri. *The Two Sources of Morality and Religion.* Translated by R. Ashley Audra and Cloudesly Brereton, with the assistance of W. Horsfall Carter. Garden City, N.Y.: Doubleday and Company, Anchor Books, 1954.

Brough, John B. "The Emergence of an Absolute Consciousness in Husserl's Early Writings on Time-Consciousness." In *Husserl: Expositions and Appraisals,* edited by Frederick Elliston and Peter McCormick, 83–100. Notre Dame: University of Notre Dame Press, 1977.

Buber, Martin. *I and Thou.* Translated by Walter Kaufmann. New York: Charles Scribner's Sons, 1970.

Bueno, Anibal A. "Consciousness, Time, and Transcendence in Eric Voegelin's Philosophy." In *The Philosophy of Order: Essays on History, Consciousness, and Politics,* edited by Peter J. Opitz and Gregor Sebba, 91–109. Stuttgart: Klett-Cotta, 1981.

Caringella, Paul. "Eric Voegelin: Philosopher of Divine Presence." *Modern Age* 34 (Spring 1990): 7–22.

Carmody, Denise Lardner, and John Tully Carmody. "Voegelin and the Restoration of Order: A Meditation." *Horizons* 14 (1987): 82–96.

Carmody, John. "Noetic Differentiation: Religious Implications." In *Voegelin and the Theologian: Ten Studies in Interpretation,* edited by John Kirby and William M. Thompson, 138–77. Toronto Studies in Theology, vol. 10. New York: The Edwin Mellen Press, 1983.

Collingwood, R. G. *The Idea of History.* Galaxy Book Edition. New York: Oxford University Press, 1963.

Cooper, Barry. *The Political Theory of Eric Voegelin.* Toronto Studies in Theology, vol. 27. Lewiston, N.Y.: The Edwin Mellen Press, 1986.

Corrington, John William. "Order and Consciousness/Consciousness and History: The New Program of Voegelin." In *Eric Voegelin's Search for Order in History,* edited by Stephen A. McKnight, 155–95. Baton Rouge: Louisiana State University Press, 1978.

Dallmayr, Fred. "Voegelin's Search for Order." *Journal of Politics* 51 (May 1989): 411–30.

Douglass, Bruce. "A Diminished Gospel: A Critique of Voegelin's Interpretation of Christianity." In *Eric Voegelin's Search for Order in History,* edited by Stephen A. McKnight, 139–54. Baton Rouge: Louisiana State University Press, 1978.

Eliade, Mircea. *Myth and Reality.* Translated by Willard R. Trask. Torchbook Edition. New York: Harper and Row, 1968.

————. *The Myth of the Eternal Return; or, Cosmos and History.* Translated by Willard R. Trask. Bollingen Series 46. Princeton: Princeton University Press, 1974.

————. *No Souvenirs: Journal, 1957–1969.* Translated by Fred H. Johnson, Jr. New York: Harper and Row, 1977.

————. *The Sacred and the Profane: The Nature of Religion.* Translated by Willard R. Trask. New York: Harcourt, Brace and World, Inc., 1959.

Eliot, T. S. *Four Quartets.* London: Faber and Faber, 1970.

Elliston, Frederick, and Peter McCormick, eds. *Husserl: Expositions and Appraisals.* Notre Dame: University of Notre Dame Press, 1977.

Fackenheim, Emil L. *Metaphysics and Historicity.* The Aquinas Lecture Series. Milwaukee: Marquette University Press, 1961.

Frankfort, Henri. *Kingship and the Gods.* Chicago: University of Chicago Press, 1948.

Frankfort, Henri, H. A. Frankfort, John A. Wilson, Thorkild Jacobsen, and William A. Irwin. *The Intellectual Adventure of Ancient Man.* Chicago: University of Chicago Press, 1977.

Gebhardt, Jürgen. "Toward the Process of Universal Mankind: The Formation of Voegelin's Philosophy of History." In *Eric Voegelin's Thought: A Critical Appraisal,* edited by Ellis Sandoz, 67–86. Durham, N.C.: Duke University Press, 1982.

Germino, Dante. "Eric Voegelin's *Anamnesis.*" *Southern Review* 7 (1971): 68–88.

————. *Political Philosophy and the Open Society.* Baton Rouge: Louisiana State University Press, 1982.

Grene, Marjorie. *A Portrait of Aristotle.* Phoenix Book Edition. Chicago: University of Chicago Press, 1973.

Guthrie, W. K. C. *The Greek Philosophers: From Thales to Aristotle.* Torchbook Edition. New York: Harper and Row, 1960.

Havard, William C. "Voegelin's Changing Conception of History and Consciousness." In *Eric Voegelin's Search for Order in History,* edited by Stephen A. McKnight, 1–25. Baton Rouge: Louisiana State University Press, 1978.

Heidegger, Martin. *Basic Writings.* Edited by David Farrell Krell. New York: Harper and Row, 1977.

————. *Being and Time.* Translated by John Macquarrie and Edward Robinson. New York: Harper and Row, 1962.

————. "Letter on Humanism." Translated by Frank A. Capuzzi in collaboration with J. Glenn Gray. In *Basic Writings,* edited by David Farrell Krell, 193–242. New York: Harper and Row, 1977.

Husserl, Edmund. *Cartesian Meditations.* Translated by Dorian Cairns. The Hague: Martinus Nijhoff, 1977.

Jaeger, Werner. *Paideia: The Ideals of Greek Culture,* vol. 1. Translated by Gilbert Highet. New York: Oxford University Press, 1960.

———. *The Theology of the Early Greek Philosophers.* Translated by Edward S. Robinson. London: Oxford University Press, 1967.

Jaspers, Karl. *The Origin and Goal of History.* Translated by Michael Bullock. London: Routledge and Kegan Paul, 1953.

Jaspers, Karl, and Rudolf Bultmann. *Myth and Christianity: An Inquiry Into the Possibility of Religion Without Myth.* Translator unnamed. New York: The Noonday Press, 1964.

Jonas, Hans. *The Gnostic Religion.* Boston: Beacon Press, 1958.

Kahn, Charles H. *The Art and Thought of Heraclitus.* Cambridge: Cambridge University Press, 1981.

Kant, Immanuel. *Critique of Practical Reason.* Translated by Lewis White Beck. Indianapolis: The Bobbs-Merrill Company, 1977.

———. *Critique of Pure Reason.* Translated by Max Müller. Garden City, N.Y.: Doubleday and Company, Anchor Books, 1966.

Kierkegaard, Søren. *The Concept of Dread.* Translated by Walter Lowrie. Princeton: Princeton University Press, 1969.

———. *The Sickness unto Death.* Edited and translated by Howard V. Hong and Edna H. Hong. Princeton: Princeton University Press, 1983.

Kirby, John. "On Reading Eric Voegelin: A Note on the Critical Literature." In *Voegelin and the Theologian: Ten Studies in Interpretation,* edited by John Kirby and William M. Thompson, 24–60. Toronto Studies in Theology, vol. 10. New York: The Edwin Mellen Press, 1983.

Kirby, John, and William M. Thompson, eds. *Voegelin and the Theologian: Ten Studies in Interpretation.* Toronto Studies in Theology, vol. 10. New York: The Edwin Mellen Press, 1983.

Kirk, G. S., and J. E. Raven. *The Presocratic Philosophers.* Cambridge: The University Press, 1964.

Kuntz, Paul G., ed. *The Concept of Order.* Seattle: University of Washington Press, 1968.

Lawrence, Frederick. "On 'The Meditative Origin of the Philosophical Knowledge of Order.'" In *The Beginning and the Beyond,* edited by Frederick Lawrence, 53–67. Chico, Calif.: Scholars Press, 1984.

————. "Voegelin and Theology as Hermeneutical and Political." In *Voegelin and the Theologian: Ten Studies in Interpretation,* edited by John Kirby and William M. Thompson, 314–55. Toronto Studies in Theology, vol. 10. New York: The Edwin Mellen Press, 1983.

————, ed. *The Beginning and the Beyond: Papers from the Gadamer and Lonergan Conferences, Supplementary Issue of Lonergan Workshop, Volume 4.* Chico, Calif.: Scholars Press, 1984.

Lonergan, Bernard J. F. *Insight: A Study of Human Understanding.* San Francisco: Harper and Row, 1978.

Löwith, Karl. *Meaning in History.* Phoenix Book Edition. Chicago: University of Chicago Press, 1964.

McKnight, Stephen A. "The Evolution of Voegelin's Theory of Politics and History, 1944–1975." In *Eric Voegelin's Search for Order in History,* edited by Stephen A. McKnight, 26–45. Baton Rouge: Louisiana State University Press, 1978.

————, ed. *Eric Voegelin's Search for Order in History.* Baton Rouge: Louisiana State University Press, 1978.

Macquarrie, John. *Mystery and Truth.* Milwaukee: Marquette University Theology Department, 1973.

Marcel, Gabriel. *Being and Having: An Existentialist Diary.* Translated by Kathleen Farrer. Torchbook Edition. New York: Harper and Row, 1965.

————. *Man Against Mass Society.* Translated by G. S. Fraser. South Bend, Indiana: Gateway Editions, 1978.

————. *The Mystery of Being.* 2 vols. Vol. 1, *Reflection and Mystery,* translated by G. S. Fraser; Vol. 2, *Faith and Reality,* translated by René Hague. Gateway Edition. Chicago: Henry Regnery Co., 1960.

Nieli, Russell. "Eric Voegelin's Evolving Ideas on Gnosticism, Mysticism, and Modern Radical Politics." *Independent Journal of Philosophy* 5–6 (1988): 93–102.

Niemeyer, Gerhart. "Eric Voegelin's Philosophy and the Drama of Mankind." *Modern Age* 20 (Winter 1976): 28–39.

————. "God and Man, World and Society: The Last Work of Eric Voegelin." *The Review of Politics* 51 (1989): 107–23.

Onians, Richard Broxton. *The Origins of European Thought.* New York: Arno Press, 1973.

Opitz, Peter J., and Gregor Sebba, eds. *The Philosophy of Order: Essays on History, Consciousness, and Politics.* Stuttgart: Klett-Cotta, 1981.

Perkins, Pheme. "Gnosis and the Life of the Spirit: The Price of Pneumatic

Order." In *Voegelin and the Theologian: Ten Studies in Interpretation,* edited by John Kirby and William M. Thompson, 222–52. Toronto Studies in Theology, vol. 10. New York: The Edwin Mellen Press, 1983.

Pieper, Josef. *Hope and History.* Translated by Richard and Clara Winston. New York: Herder and Herder, 1969.

Plato. *Collected Dialogues of Plato.* Edited by Edith Hamilton and Huntington Cairns. Princeton: Princeton University Press, 1973.

———. *Philebus.* Translated by R. Hackforth. In *Collected Dialogues of Plato,* edited by Edith Hamilton and Huntington Cairns, 1086–1150. Princeton: Princeton University Press, 1973.

———. *The Republic of Plato.* Translated by Allan Bloom. New York: Basic Books, Inc., 1968.

———. *Symposium.* Translated by Michael Joyce. In *Collected Dialogues of Plato,* edited by Edith Hamilton and Huntington Cairns, 526–74. Princeton: Princeton University Press, 1973.

———. *Timaeus.* Translated by Benjamin Jowett. In *Collected Dialogues of Plato,* edited by Edith Hamilton and Huntington Cairns, 1151–1211. Princeton: Princeton University Press, 1973.

Polanyi, Michael, and Harry Prosch. *Meaning.* Chicago: University of Chicago Press, 1975.

Rahner, Karl. *Foundations of Christian Faith.* Translated by William V. Dych. New York: The Seabury Press, 1978.

Richardson, William J. *Heidegger: Through Phenomenology to Thought.* The Hague: Martinus Nijhoff, 1963.

Rosen, Stanley. *Plato's Symposium.* New Haven: Yale University Press, 1987.

Sandoz, Ellis. *The Voegelinian Revolution: A Biographical Introduction.* Baton Rouge: Louisiana State University Press, 1981.

———, ed. *Eric Voegelin's Thought: A Critical Appraisal.* Durham, N.C.: Duke University Press, 1982.

Scheler, Max. *Man's Place in Nature.* Translated by Hans Meyerhoff. Boston: Beacon Press, 1961.

Sebba, Gregor. "History, Modernity, and Gnosticism." In *The Philosophy of Order: Essays on History, Consciousness, and Politics,* edited by Peter J. Opitz and Gregor Sebba, 190–241. Stuttgart: Klett-Cotta, 1981.

———. "Prelude and Variations on the Theme of Eric Voegelin." In *Eric Voegelin's Thought: A Critical Appraisal,* edited by Ellis Sandoz, 3–65. Durham, N.C.: Duke University Press, 1982.

Steiner, George. *Real Presences.* Chicago: University of Chicago Press, 1989.

Webb, Eugene. *Eric Voegelin: Philosopher of History*. Seattle: University of Washington Press, 1981.

———. "Eric Voegelin's Theory of Revelation." In *Eric Voegelin's Thought: A Critical Appraisal*, edited by Ellis Sandoz, 157–78. Durham, N.C.: Duke University Press, 1982.

———. "Metaphysics or Existenzerhellung: A Comparison of Lonergan and Voegelin." *Religious Studies and Theology* 7 (May/September 1987): 36–47.

———. *Philosophers of Consciousness: Polanyi, Lonergan, Voegelin, Ricoeur, Girard, Kierkegaard*. Seattle: University of Washington Press, 1988.

Weiss, Raymond L. "Voegelin's Biblical Hermeneutics." *Independent Journal of Philosophy* 5–6 (1988): 81–84.

INDEX

Abraham, 51
Analogy, 30–31, 46, 47, 66–67, 90, 110; myth as, 9–10, 109
Anaxagoras, 26
Anaximander, 48n10
Aquinas, Saint Thomas, 27, 57–58
Aristotle, 45, 60, 92–93 passim; and Plato as first analysts of consciousness, 12, 23–24; Voegelin's reliance on terms of, 26–27; and notion of participation, 27–29; and myth, 35
Attunement, 74, 75–76, 81–84, 97, 98, 103; definition of, 81–82
Augustine, Saint, 16, 70, 78

Balance of consciousness, 102–3, 104
Beginning, the. *See* Beyond, the; Ground, the
Being: primordial community of, 45; symbol of, 51
Bergson, Henri, 61
Beyond, the: experience of, 18–19; category of, 52–54; and the Beginning, 67–69, 90–91, 100, 103; acknowledged in a convincing myth, 86–87; and the struggle for attunement, 97–99; and gnosticism, 100. *See also* Ground, the; Transcendence
Bossuet, Jacques Bénigne, 70
Brentano, Franz, 34
Buddha, Buddhism, 43, 78

Christ. *See* Jesus
Christianity, 59, 76
Coincidentia oppositorum, 5, 30
Compact consciousness. *See* Con-

sciousness; Differentiation of consciousness
Comte, Auguste, 14
Confucius, 43, 78
Consciousness: as participation, 4–5, 28–33, 113–16 passim; as subject and non-subject, 4–5, 11–13, 20–22, 34–37, 110–12; as given, 5, 13, 14, 82, 113–15; reification of, 5, 12, 93; as questioning awareness, 7–8, 24–26, 28, 60–61; misinterpretation of, 12; historical dimension of, 13–15, 21; aware of being constituted by reality, 14, 113–14; as luminosity, 15, 19–20, 22, 34–38, 40, 105–7, 110–12, 116; transcendent dimension of, 15–19, 20–21, 93–95; rooted in bodily processes, 16, 17; as intersection of timeless with time, 16, 16n12, 22, 32–33, 93–94; as stratum in unfolding of reality, 19–20, 80–81; as in-between (*metaxy*), 24, 28–29, 29n32, 74, 93–95; as the Question, 24–26, 41–42; as human and divine, 26–33, 92–94; as divine-human encounter, 29n32, 33; intentional vs. luminous, 34–37; structures of, 34–37, 111–12; compact, 38–39, 42, 45–48, 52 (*see also* Differentiation of consciousness); as locus of discovery of transcendence, 53–54; desire to know as core of, 60–61; emergence of historical, 75–76, 76n9; eschatological, 97–98, 99, 101–2; balance of, 102–3, 104; as event in Being, 105–6; mystery as a dimension of, 105–7; able to out-question the knowable, 105–8; imbalanced, 107. *See also* Balance of consciousness; Differentia-